D1221420

0026656

THE
GREAT COMPOSERS
THEIR LIVES AND TIMES

Hector
Berlioz
1803-1869

Felix
Mendelssohn
1809-1847

Robert
Schumann
1810-1856

Staff Credits

Editors
David Buxton BA (Honours)
Sue Lyon BA (Honours)

Art Editors
Debbie Jecock BA (Honours)
Ray Leaning BA (Honours),
PGCE (Art & Design)

Deputy Editor
Barbara Segall BA

Sub-editors
Geraldine Jones
Judy Oliver BA (Honours)
Nigel Rodgers BA (Honours), MA
Penny Smith
Will Steeds BA (Honours), MA

Designers
Steve Chilcott BA (Honours)
Shirin Patel BA (Honours)
Chris Rathbone

Picture Researchers
Georgina Barker
Julia Calloway BA (Honours)
Vanessa Cawley

Production Controllers
Sue Fuller
Steve Roberts

Secretary
Lynn Smail

Publisher
Terry Waters Grad IOP

Editorial Director
Maggi McCormick

Production Executive
Robert Paulley BSc

Managing Editor
Alan Ross BA (Honours)

Consultants
Dr Antony Hopkins
Commander of the Order
of the British Empire,
Fellow of the
Royal College of Music

Nick Mapstone BA (Honours), MA

Keith Shadwick BA (Honours)

Reference Edition Published 1987

Published by Marshall Cavendish Corporation
147 West Merrick Road
Freeport, Long Island
N.Y. 11520

Typeset by Walkergate Press Ltd, Hull, England
Printed and Bound in Singapore by
Koon Wah Printing Pte Ltd.

© Marshall Cavendish Limited MCMLXXXIV,
MCMLXXXVII

Library of Congress Cataloging-in-Publication Data

The Great composers, their lives and times.

   Includes index.
   1. Composers—Biography.   2. Music appreciation.
I. Marshall Cavendish Corporation.
ML390.G82   1987   780'.92'2 [B]   86-31294
ISBN 0-86307-776-5

ISBN 0-86307-776-5 (set)
   0-86307-784-6 (vol)

THE GREAT COMPOSERS
THEIR LIVES AND TIMES

Hector
Berlioz
1803-1869

Felix
Mendelssohn
1809-1847

Robert
Schumann
1810-1856

MARSHALL CAVENDISH
NEW YORK · LONDON · SYDNEY

Contents

Introduction

The romantic image of the artist who suffers mentally and physically for his art, or who is overwhelmed by passion for his beloved, is now a cliché. In some ways, the lives of the three composers in this volume – Hector Berlioz, Felix Mendelssohn and Robert Schumann – conform to this stereotype. Berlioz's most famous work, the Symphonie Fantastique, was composed as a result of his passion for the actress Harriet Smithson, while Schumann ended his life in a lunatic asylum. Even that debonair gentleman, Felix Mendelssohn, was passionately – some historians suggest dangerously – attached to his sister Fanny.

The extremes of these composers' lives should not, however, blind us to their achievements. All three men were serious artists, whose works are some of the greatest expressions of the Romantic spirit. To varying degrees, they influenced their contemporaries and those composers that followed; Berlioz had less impact than Mendelssohn or Schumann since he was too much of a maverick to attract followers or imitators. Even without the music that they wrote, all three men would be notable for their contribution to the history of music. Mendelssohn was responsible for the revival of interest in the works of J. S. Bach and Handel; Berlioz's Treatise on Modern Instrumentation and Orchestration was the first of its kind and remains a standard work today; and Schumann was an influential music critic who championed both the works of earlier composers like Scarlatti, Gluck and Couperin, and the music of contemporaries like Chopin – whom he hailed as a genius – and the young Brahms.

THE GREAT COMPOSERS

Hector Berlioz

1803-1869

With his overwhelming passions, violent swings of mood and wild appearance, Hector Berlioz was the archetypal Romantic artist. Although he has been described as the greatest French composer of the 19th century, he has always been more admired outside his native land. During his life-time, opinions were mixed: Liszt was entranced by his music, while Mendelssohn described him as a total freak who was devoid of talent. The Symphonie Fantastique *– Berlioz's most famous composition – is analyzed in the* Listener's Guide. *At first sight a work of highly coloured bombast, it in fact contains passages of lyrical beauty that display the intensity of love that caused Berlioz to write the symphony. Scorned by his compatriots, Berlioz found greater appreciation abroad, especially in Britain which he visited in 1851 at the time of the Great Exhibition. As In the* Background *describes, this was perhaps the zenith of the Victorian age, when the world came to London, the capital of industrially mighty Britain, the 'workshop of the world'.*

COMPOSER'S LIFE

'A total freak'

Throughout his stormy, uneasy life he was labelled a genius by some, reviled as an untalented freak by others. Possibly the most original Romantic composer, Hector Berlioz was driven by a unique musical vision that went far beyond his time.

Lauros–Giraudon

Lauros–Giraudon

Born into a respectable, religious country family, Berlioz showed his extraordinary temperament at an early age. At 12 he fell in love with Estelle, a girl of 18, becoming so obsessed with her that, whenever she was near, he felt physically ill. He learnt to play three instruments and, by 16, (right) was sending his compositions to Paris publishers. But his father (above), a doctor, refused to let him study music; at 18 he was sent away to medical school in Paris.

Scala

To Hector Berlioz, possibly the most original Romantic composer and conductor, music was 'a heavenly art'. He declared that: 'Nothing surpasses it, but true love. The one will always make me as unhappy as the other but, at least, I shall have lived.'

The way he lived, with a fiery temperament and perverse delight in provocation, alienated many of his contemporaries. Mendelssohn thought him 'a total freak, without a vestige of talent.' Others, like his close friend Liszt, were entranced by his enthusiasm and unpredictability. They found him delightful, even child-like, and revelled in his devilish sense of humour. Much impressed, the German poet Heine

called Berlioz 'an immense nightingale; a lark as great as an eagle'.

All his life Berlioz struggled against bankruptcy, being forced to work as a music journalist for a living. Public opposition to his works and personality in his native France meant that he went largely un-appreciated, despite having such a profound influence in other countries that he is often considered the father of modern orchestration.

Berlioz would whip himself into emotional frenzies, alternately unable to work, then rushing into a stream of tireless composition and study. His violent swings of mood, combined with rejections and material difficulties, produced an unprecedented directness of passion in his music, but left him an embittered old man who died alone, and chronically ill.

Yet this excessively Romantic figure was also a professional who demanded exacting standards of himself in all that he did. One of the greatest musical innovators, he was grandiloquent, unclassifiable and eccentric: a true maverick of his time.

The serious child

Louis Hector Berlioz was born on 11 December, 1803, at La Côte-St. André, in the district of Dauphiné. His father was a much-loved country doctor and his mother a pious, orthodox Roman Catholic. This religion, which Berlioz described as 'so attractive, since it gave up burning people', kept its place in his affections even though he publicly mocked it for most of his life. Berlioz's father was his principal teacher in childhood, instructing him in Latin, classical literature and rudimentary medicine, the profession he hoped his son would follow. The boy was encouraged to take up music, but only as an educational hobby. He played the flute, guitar and recorder rather well, but showed little interest in the piano at this stage. Berlioz seems to have been a rather sensitive and impressionable child; in his highly entertaining *Memoirs* he recalls that, at the age of seven, when translating a passage from Virgil's *Aeneid,* he was overcome by a nervous shuddering. At 12 he discovered his two majestic and fateful passions: music and love. Estelle, a neighbour's niece, was 18. The moment Berlioz set eyes on her, he later wrote, he felt an electric shock, and then

Berlioz's childhood home (left) was a stable, comfortable environment that nurtured his many talents. But Paris, a mecca for artists and musicians, was his true milieu. He soon became known for his fiery personality and strange, intense appearance. His friend Legouve described him at the time: 'his eyes blazing... and a head of hair like an immense umbrella or movable canopy overhanging the beak of a bird of prey... at once comical and diabolical!'

'suffered acutely and spent my nights in sleepless anguish'. Each subsequent encounter left him feeling worse, but he never forgot the power of his first love.

He began composing in the same period, and by 16 he was offering his works, unsuccessfully, to Paris publishers. But his father, refusing to believe that his son was serious about music, eventually packed him off to Paris to study medicine.

A musical vocation

The Paris of the 1820s was, to the young Berlioz, an artistic and musical paradise that made medical school most unappealing. At first, horrified by the sight of the dissecting room, he jumped out of the window and fled. Later, he developed a bored detachment from it, amusing himself by feeding pieces of cadavers to the birds. Respecting his father's wishes (and dependent on his money), he kept up his studies for several years, but his musical ambitions gradually took complete control of him. He became a regular at the Paris Opéra; there, seized by the music of Gluck, he felt that short of fainting he could have had no greater experience. He read and copied Gluck's scores in the library: 'An ecstasy possessed me... I went without sleep because of them, and forgot to eat or drink', he wrote. He

abandoned the dissecting room and, on submitting some compositions to the composer Lesueur, was accepted as a private pupil.

Berlioz's father took violent exception. He condemned the musical profession, and Madame Berlioz felt sure it would lead to her son's damnation. In fury, Berlioz wrote to them that: 'I would rather be Gluck or Mehul dead than what I am in the flower of my manhood . . .' His father relented, allowing him to study music for a trial period; if he failed he was to return to medicine, or take up some other respectable profession.

In 1826, the Paris Conservatoire admitted Berlioz, by then 23. He wrote an opera, then a Mass which, as no one else would perform it, he staged himself with borrowed money. Desperate to pay back the loan he gave music lessons, but couldn't earn enough. Unfortunately his father heard of the affair and was outraged by such extravagance. He settled the debt on Berlioz's behalf, as a matter of honour, but then cut off his son's allowance altogether. Berlioz, more certain than ever of his vocation following his teacher's approval of the Mass, decided to go it alone. But with the coming of winter in 1825, he found himself cold and his clothes threadbare. Needing extra income, he

Bored by medical school, Berlioz began to spend his time at concerts, the opera and the theatre, drawing inspiration from Shakespeare, and Beethoven, Gluck and the many other 'greats' of his time. Romantic theatre usually portrayed its characters in the grip of uncontrollable passions (left), and Berlioz was indeed like this himself.

became a singer in the vaudeville chorus of the Théâtre des Nouveautés. Although the inanity of the music he had to perform almost drove him mad, Berlioz coped with this, and the strains of overwork, until his father, eventually, agreed to support his prodigal son again.

Paris and Rome

The years 1827–30 were certainly Berlioz's most formative. Twice, he fell hopelessly in love. His work began to receive critical acclaim and, on the fourth attempt, he won the coveted music scholarship, the Prix de Rome.

Berlioz adored Shakespeare and went eagerly to see a season of plays, presented in Paris in 1827 by the English actor Charles Kemble. Appearing in *Hamlet,* as Ophelia, was the Irish actress Harriet Smithson. Her performance enraptured most of theatre-going Paris; Berlioz himself was overcome, as maddened by her beauty as he had been by Estelle's. He bombarded her with love letters, but so frightened was she by such unrestrained passion that she finally refused to accept any more. Berlioz despaired.

Torn by his feelings for Harriet, he launched into the *Symphonie Fantastique,* a musical dramatization of his elaborate grief. Despite offending some critics with its bizarre death sequence, the piece was fairly well received when first performed in December 1830. The composition seemed to get Harriet out of Berlioz's system, for a time. He wrote to his friend Humbert Ferrand: 'I am no longer in danger from that quarter . ... I pity and despise her.' Later in the same

Mauro Pucciarelli

Courtesy of the Victoria & Albert Museum

year, he fell in love with Camille Moke, a particularly gifted young pianist.

Inspired, like most composers at this time, by the German poet Goethe, Berlioz also composed *Eight Scenes from Faust.* He sent a copy of the score to the master, with a most effusive letter. But Goethe did not reply: his musical advisor told him *Faust* was a work of 'coughs, snores, croakings and expectorations.' Berlioz's first pieces submitted for the Prix de Rome, met a similar reaction from the judges. But his final attempt, *Death of Sardanapalus,* based on a Delacroix painting, won him the award unanimously.

This proved a mixed blessing as it included a period of compulsory study in Rome. Berlioz left Paris unwillingly as, after overcoming severe parental opposition, he had just become engaged to Camille. Rome precipitated another emotional crisis; not hearing from his fiancée, he started back to Paris within weeks. But before he reached the French border, a letter from Camille's mother told him that she had married someone else. Spurned in love once again, Berlioz records in his *Memoirs* his reaction to this 'odious crime'. He would return to Paris, disguised as a lady's maid, packing a pair of pistols and bottles of strychnine and laudanum. Having murdered Camille and her mother, he would then kill himself. Stopping en route in Nice for a meal though, his mood abruptly changed. Instead, he stayed there, composed the overture to *King Lear,* then went back to Italy. For the next 12 months he did little except acquire a love of the Italian countryside, which later inspired his *Harold in Italy.*

During his stay he met Mendelssohn, and together they explored the local ruins. Mendelssohn was a religious man and Berlioz taunted him mercilessly. On one occasion, both of them poised on a steep, ruined staircase, Berlioz made some heretical remarks. Mendelssohn lost his footing, falling to the ground

C'est seulement ainsi que les grandes compositions complexes de l'art musical peuvent être sauvées et garanties de la morsure des rats qui grouillent dans les théâtres, dans les théâtres de France, d'Angleterre, d'Italie, d'Allemagne même, de partout. Car il ne faut pas se faire illusion, les théâtres lyriques sont tous les mêmes ; ce sont les mauvais lieux de la musique, et la chaste muse qu'on y traîne ne peut y entrer qu'en frémissant. Pourquoi cela ? Oh ! nous le savons trop, on l'a trop souvent dit, il n'y a nul besoin de le redire. Répétons seulement ici, pour la vingtième fois au moins, et à propos de la récente reproduction à l'Opéra, d'une œuvre pareille ne pourra être dignement exécutée, que sous la surveillance d'un artiste dévoué parfaitement maître de toutes les questions qui se rattachent à la musique et aux études musicales, profondément pénétré de tout ce qu'il y a de grand et de beau dans l'art, et qui, jouissant d'une autorité justifiée par son caractère, ses connaissances spéciales et l'élévation de ses vues, l'exercerait tantôt avec douceur, tantôt avec une rigidité absolue ; qui ne connaîtrait ni amis ni ennemis ; un Brutus l'ancien qui, une fois ses ordres donnés et les voyant transgressés, serait toujours prêt à dire : *I lictor, liga ad palum !* « Va, licteur, lie au poteau le coupable ! » — Mais c'est M. ***, c'est Mlle ***, c'est Mme ***. — *I lictor !* » Vous demandez l'établissement du despotisme dans les théâtres ? me dira-t-on. Et je répondrai : Oui, dans les théâtres lyriques surtout, et dans les établissemens qui ont pour objet d'obtenir un beau résultat musical au moyen d'un personnel nombreux d'exécutans de divers ordres, obligés de concourir à un seul et même but, il faut le despotisme, souverainement intelligent sans doute, mais le despotisme enfin, le despotisme militaire, le despotisme d'un général en chef, d'un amiral en temps de guerre. Hors de là il n'y a que résultats incomplets, contre-sens, désordre et cacophonie.

qu'une œuvre de la nature d'alceste ne sera jamais dignement exécutée que sous la surveillance d'un artiste dévoué qui connaît parfaitement, depuis longtemps familier avec le style du maître, possédant à fond

below. Picking him up, Berlioz declared: 'There's an example of divine justice for you. I blaspheme, you fall'. Mendelssohn decided never to discuss religion with him again.

'My Thirty Years War'

Back in Paris in 1832, Berlioz found himself still penniless, facing strong opposition and a battle to consolidate his reputation. Harriet was back too, this time running a theatrical company that soon fell into debt. After a performance of the now revised *Symphonie Fantastique,* the two met. Berlioz's reawakened passion for her was reciprocated. They had a stormy affair. At one time Harriet accused him of not loving her; exasperated, he decided to make her regret it by taking poison in front of her. In a letter to his friend Humbert, he described her reaction to this macabre piece of melodrama:

Dreadful cries . . . (her despair was sublime) – fiendish laughter on my part – desire to live again on seeing her prostestation of love – emetics . . . vomiting for two hours . . . I was ill for three days but I survived.

They married on October 3, 1833, and had a son, Louis, 10 months later. Berlioz later described the period from then until his retirement as 'My thirty years war against . . . academics and the deaf.' Although *Harold* was received quite well, and the government commissioned him, in 1837, to write his *Requiem,* his opera *Benvenuto Cellini* was reviled and the cost of its production cast him further into debt. He was saved

Berlioz continued to compose and conduct, but his unorthodox style made him a sitting target for the cartoonists of the time (above left).

In Hamlet, *as Ophelia, the actress Harriet Smithson (left) overwhelmed Berlioz. The moment he saw her he fell hopelessly in love.*

Despite parental opposition, Berlioz became a music student, eventually winning a scholarship to study in Rome. He hated the place, but the surrounding villages (right) and countryside greatly inspired his later work. Back in Paris, short of money, he was forced to become a music critic for a living, which he loathed. In his Memoirs *he describes what he went through to deliver a piece of copy (above). 'I . . . do anything to fight off the boredom and fatigue . . . It can take eight or nine attempts before I am rid of an article . . . And then the blots and the scratchings-out! The first draft looks like a battlefield.'*

only by a gift of 20,000 francs, probably from Paganini, the virtuoso violinist, himself a notorious eccentric. He used the money to compose *Romeo and Juliet,* which proved highly successful.

Despite incessant work, however, Berlioz's earnings from 1832–42 did not exceed $2,800 at present value. He needed, as other composers had, a professorship or major conductorship, but these were denied him. The Paris Opéra, which paid extraordinarily high royalties to composers, consistently rejected his works. So music criticism for the *Journal des Débats* remained his mainstay, depriving him of valuable composition time. As one would expect, Berlioz was a caustic, provocative writer whose pieces won him a select following. But they also show just how he disagreed with the musical standards of his time; in every sense, he fought an uphill battle with his contemporaries. His reputation in France began to slide. Nonetheless, throughout his 30s, he composed prolifically, became a figure of European repute, and lost none of his youthful fire and panache. An account of the time describes a performance of his *Symphonie Funèbre et Triomphale* in the open air. Confronted by a full orchestra and brass band of 200, Berlioz conducted with a drawn sword, collapsing at the end across the kettle drums, weeping.

By this time, Harriet was weeping as well. After six years, their marriage was in ruins. When Berlioz went to Germany two years later he had a lover, the singer and actress Marie Recio. Two years later, he left Harriet for good.

Subsequent trips throughout Europe were enormously successful for Berlioz; acclaimed and materially provided for by his hosts, he was to keep travelling for the next 25 years. In London, in 1846, he accepted an invitation to conduct opera at the Drury Lane Theatre, but unfortunately the concert manager ran off with the funds and Berlioz was forced back to Paris. The city, in the throes of the 1848 uprising, was not a welcoming musical environment, so Berlioz soon returned to London for The Great Exhibition of 1851. His music continued to get mixed reactions, but throughout the 40s and 50s Berlioz established himself as an author of repute. He published his *Treatise on Modern Instrumentation and Orchestration,* the first book of its kind and one which remains a standard text today, began his *Memoirs* and issued a collection of his journalism.

Age and despair
Despite his successes and international prominence, Berlioz did not win his self-proclaimed struggle

Berlioz was never really accepted in France, but became an acclaimed musical figure throughout England and the rest of Europe in the 1840s and 50s. Most of his works were composed during this time, but it was towards the end of his life that he wrote The Trojans, *based on Virgil's heroic tale of Dido and Aeneas (above). He had wrestled all his life with how best to pay tribute to it in music, and for him it was his greatest work. But the opera companies of Europe refused to stage it except in a bastardized form. Berlioz considered this an insult, and became deeply depressed.*

against the French musical establishment. After his 50th year, a series of losses and setbacks gradually wore him down, defusing his once volatile spirit. The first of these was Harriet's death in 1854. Despite their separation, Berlioz grieved deeply. He married Marie soon after, and finished his *Memoirs,* but his health started to fail and within three years he was suffering an acute intestinal disorder that made him miserable.

He started his monumental work, *The Trojans* (based on the *Aeneid*), which took more than a year to finish. Then, no-one would perform it, except in a drastically cut version in 1863 which Berlioz called a 'ridiculous travesty'. Ironically, this brought him accolades, enthusiastic reviews and money, but to Berlioz it was the crowning insult to all his years of effort. He completed his last work, *Beatrice and Benedict,* but with Marie's death, decided to compose no longer. Also resigning his post on the *Journal des Débats,* he wrote:

I am ... past hopes, past illusions, past high thoughts and lofty conceptions. My contempt for the folly and baseness of mankind, my hatred of its atrocious cruelty have never been more intense. And I say hourly to death: 'When you will'.

In an attempt to revive himself, he sought out his first love, Estelle. By then a 67-year-old widow, she was bewildered by this intense old man who said he had loved her for 50 years, but eventually agreed to write to him. Otherwise, prematurely aged and deeply depressed, Berlioz withdrew from the world. Tormented by the increasing pain in his bowels, he took larger and larger doses of laudanum which left him dazed and stupid. Then, in 1865, his son Louis died of yellow fever in Havana. He found one last pleasure in a conducting trip to Russia, where he left a lasting impression on Rimsky-Korsakov and the other young composers there.

After his return to Paris, the death of his life-long friend Humbert proved the final blow. Berlioz died on March 8, 1869. According to accounts by his friends, Berlioz died tragically believing that his genius had been an illusion; that in death, his name and works would disappear forever. In this, thankfully, he was proved wrong.

The rejection of The Trojans, *and a worsening chronic illness, turned Berlioz (below right) into a bitter, unhappy old man who wished only to die as soon as possible. After his wife Harriet died, he married Marie Recio (above, right). But when she too died Berlioz gave up composing and shut himself away. In his despair he reached out to his first love Estelle, now an old woman whom he had not seen for many years. The letters that she subsequently wrote him, and a trip to Moscow (above) where he was almost idolized by young composers, were the only pleasures of his last years. He died, believing his whole life had been a mistake, in 1869, aged 66.*

LISTENER'S GUIDE

Symphonie Fantastique, op. 14

Unrequited love, opium, suicide, the guillotine and a monstrous Witches' Sabbath, are some of the lurid ingredients of Berlioz's Symphonie Fantastique.

Mauro Pucciarelli

The earliest authenticated portrait of Berlioz (above), signed and dated 1830, the year he wrote his extravagant Symphonie Fantastique.

'Episode in the Life of an Artist.' This is the title given by Berlioz to his *Symphonie Fantastique,* and there is no doubt that the artist concerned is meant to be the composer himself, the episode a fanciful extension of his own experiences.

In 1827 Berlioz had discovered 'the madness and melancholy' of *Hamlet* and the charms of Harriet Smithson in the role of Ophelia. And if the play struck his dramatic sensibilities a powerful blow, the actress 'wrought havoc' in his heart. Unfortunately, his approaches to Miss Smithson — whose moving performances were the talk of Paris — went unheeded. To be fair to the lady, Berlioz's letters expressing admiration and undying love comprised only a fraction of the proposals — both honourable and otherwise — that she received, and she could not have known that this 24-year-old composer was so earnest and persistent that he would eventually become her husband. Even his attempt to interest her by mounting a concert of his own music at his own expense was unsuccessful.

To have any dealings with her in real life, then, appeared impossible, so, since he was bursting with frustration, he would deal with her in music. In February, 1830 he concocted a romantic tale of his unreciprocated love and its tragic consequences for the lady and for himself, and within two months the *Symphonie Fantastique* was substantially complete. Its programme may seem unnecessarily maudlin and gory, but there can be no denying the immense skill and imagination with which the young Berlioz carried it out.

The work was first performed on 5 December, 1830, at the Paris Conservatoire of Music under the bâton of François-Antoine Habeneck, The thinly-disguised identity of Harriet Smithson in the *idée fixe* had been pierced by the Parisian gossip-mongers, and the relatively unknown composer's treatment of their heroine doubtless intrigued the concert-going public. Furthermore, the programme was handed out to the audience, leaving room for doubt only in the densest listener. The symphony was a great success. Its March was encored (the Paris audience apparently having developed a voracious taste for blood in the decades since 1789), there was applause at the end, and reviews the following day were most favourable. 'Bizarre' and 'monstrous' wrote *Figaro,* which is not only nothing less than the truth but also precisely the qualities the public craved.

Before we embark on the semi-autobiographical drama Berlioz has prepared for us, it is necessary to point out some things to remember as it unfolds.

Firstly, the *Symphonie Fantastique* as Berlioz conceived it is only half a work. It is the first part of what today we would call a multi-media event. The audience is expected to sit in a theatre for some 50 minutes with the curtain down while the symphony is played through. Then the curtain rises and the symphony's sequel, *Lélio,* is performed by orchestra with vocalists and chorus and narrator. The impractical nature of such a presentation is

Like Berlioz's Symphonie Fantastique, Delacroix's painting (right) is an 'orgy' of passions, charged with sensuality and bloodshed. Indeed, Berlioz's rich orchestral textures are almost a translation into sound of Delacroix's harmonies of colour.

Throughout the Symphony, the artist, under the influence of an opium-inspired dream, is haunted by an image of his beloved (the actress Harriet Smithson, with whom Berlioz was infatuated). She becomes inextricably associated with a musical melody, an idée fixe, which appears to torment the artist in every movement. Rossetti's painting (right) immortalizes his beloved – Lizzy Siddal – with similar intensity.

obvious, and the *Symphonie Fantastique* is today always given on its own.

Secondly, the programme devised for the symphony was something quite new in its day. Love invariably found its way onto the operatic stage, but to write a symphony dealing so explicitly with a man's feelings for a woman bordered on the permissive.

Thirdly, the events depicted are supposed to take place in an opium-inspired dream.

Fourthly, this is the first symphony by a prominent composer to employ an *idée fixe,* or fixed idea, in every movement. It is an easily-recognized melody representing the composer's beloved, and it is modified each time to fit the context.

Finally, although the end of the symphony is calculated to bring cheers from the audience, it will be seen from the composer's programme that it does not represent the time-honoured happy ending. Far from it! That requirement was taken care of in *Lélio,* subtitled 'A Return to Life'. It is worth stating that in his original sketch of the programme for this work, the finale was intended to be 'a vision of a night of revelry'. There was no mention of witches; only when his love turned sour was the intended gaiety changed to a scene of horror.

Our examination of each movement is prefaced with an abbreviated version of Berlioz's own programme note.

Programme notes

First movement: largo-allegro agitato e appassionato assai

Reveries – Passions. I take as my subject an artist blest with sensibility and a lively imagination ... who meets a woman who awakens in him for the first time his heart's desire. He falls desperately in love with her. Curiously, the image of his beloved is linked inseparably with a musical idea representing her graceful and noble character. This idée fixe *haunts him throughout the symphony.*

The slow introduction, *Largo* ('broad'), begins with one flute and one clarinet.

Other woodwind quickly join in and, together with four horns, play a quiet chord which seems already to bring a halt. But violins, muted, play a wistful, hesitating melody which gradually gains in power. At a minor climax, cellos contribute a disturbed oscillating phrase, and then pizzicato (plucked) double basses sound a word of warning. Suddenly, violins flare into action, and the rest of the strings, plus horns and bassoons, bring about a more intense climax. This quickly evaporates. Berlioz's reveries are indeed disturbed: as the violin theme, now unmuted, develops under agitated woodwind figures, a strange atmosphere of foreboding sweeps mistily around the music. Gradually these doubts are dispelled. A romantic solo horn melody becomes a yearning horn duet, before woodwind and horn chords and trembling strings swell, then recede and swell again, to give way to the fast section.

Marked *Allegro agitato e appassionato assai* (fast, agitated and extremely passionate), this commences with punctuating chords that prepare the way for the *idée fixe,* a melody no less than 40 bars in length on flute and first violins in unison. It is possible to give only the beginning of this noble theme:

Example 1.

A passionate outburst ensues during which this vitally important melody is referred to several times on violins alternating with woodwind. At one point the woodwind return briefly to the pulsating figure heard earlier on lower strings.

But a phrase (b) growing out of the first two bars (a) of Example 1 presses the music urgently forward:

Example 2

Because of its brevity, the exposition section is repeated.

At the start of the development section, the lower strings take (a) and repeat it over and over as it gradually rises in pitch, while woodwind cry out passionately. A fierce rhythmic figure for strings releases the woodwind's cry of (b), immediately echoed by strings. There follows another slowly rising figure of pounding strings under further anguished cries from woodwind, now joined by horns. This reaches an abrupt halt and three whole bars of total silence.

Now, over a disturbed accompaniment

Understanding music: programme music

Berlioz's *Symphonie Fantastique* was an innovative piece of music in many ways. One of the most remarkable innovations was the fact that he distributed a programme to the audience before the performance, giving a detailed account of the sequence of events embodied in the music. Spohr had done the same earlier with his opera *Faust* (1816), but nothing of the kind had ever happened in purely instrumental music to quite the same extent. This programme is crucial to a full appreciation of the work, and so Berlioz's symphony is often regarded as the first major example of Romantic *programme music.*

The term 'programme music' was invented by Liszt, and so is properly a

Beethoven's **Pastoral** *is a vivid example of programme music reflecting scenes of country life musically just as this painting depicts winter visually.*

Romantic term. Some people apply the term very loosely to descriptive music of any kind – that is, any music that illustrates an idea, a literary theme, a scene, or even paints a musical picture of a person. Descriptive music of this type has been heard ever since instruments were first played. Imitations of natural sounds, from waves on the shore to cockerels crowing, abound in music of all ages. And in the Renaissance full length pieces depicting a battle, such as William Byrd's *Battel,* a fifteen-section suite for harpsichord (1596), were common.

By the end of the 17th century, however, pieces of music begin to emerge that at first sight seem to fulfil Liszt's requirement that to be programme music the listener needs to know something of the scene or events described to fully understand the piece. In this sense, Vivaldi's *Four Seasons* (1725), each season preceded by a descriptive poem, is programmatic – so too are Joseph Kuhnau's *Bible Pieces* – sonatas written as early as 1700 which describe such scenes as David slaying Goliath. The crowning example, and the inspiration to the Romantics, was Beethoven's 'Pastoral' Symphony (no. 6), with its four movements each depicting a facet of rural life.

But in the Romantic era, there was a fundamental change in attitudes to music, which gave programme music far greater significance – and indeed makes the term seem inappropriate for the earlier pieces. Musicians began to see the creation of music not as an end in itself but as a vehicle for self-expression – so music must be full of meaning. There was a widening rift between *absolute music* – music written for its own sake – and programme music, which was essentially music written to express a non-musical idea.

Liszt used the concept of a programme simply to guide listeners to the correct interpretation of the music; his programmes are never narratives.

Other composers took a far more literal approach. In the *Symphonie Fantastique,* for example, the description is detailed right down to the moment the hero catches sight of his beloved across the ballroom, or the gruesome bounce of his head after execution. In Richard Strauss's *Ein Heldenleben,* we hear a goat bleating distinctly.

In the hands of lesser composers, however, programme music could often degenerate into a substitute for genuine creativity – a composer would simply take a famous piece of literature and write crudely illustrative music. This, more than anything, gave Romantic programme music a bad name, and in the early 20th century, composers began to abandon the idea and musicologists came to think of programme music as inferior to absolute music. Only in the 60s was this attitude eventually reconsidered. Composers are beginning to write programme music once more.

Fantin Latour's ballroom scene (above) was inspired by the second movement of the Symphonie Fantastique. *The 'artist' is instantly recognizable as Berlioz himself.*

the *idée fixe* returns complete: the recapitulation section has arrived. This covers much the same ground as before but with radical differences in orchestration and thematic detail, including a brief engagement with *fugato* (several overlapping statements) of (b). Soon the music quietens, and over a soft drum roll played with sponge-headed sticks (one of several novel instrumental effects Berlioz introduced in the work), the music

meditates on what has gone before. Perhaps Berlioz remembers that the exposition had contained no real second subject, for he makes amends now with a long and soulful oboe melody, very nearly as long as the *idée fixe* itself and clearly its close relation. However, this is swamped in a rising tide of passion, and the *idée fixe* returns, coarsened by its transfer to a cornet (no-one had used this instrument in a symphony before!). This reaches a tortured double climax amid off-beat timpani and swirling strings. In the coda there is still no escape from the *idée fixe;* finally the artist seems to turn for consolation to the church.

Second movement: Valse – Allegro non troppo

A Ball. The artist attends a ball, but the gaiety and festive tumult fail to distract him. The idée fixe *returns to torture him further.*

The rustle of gowns, the carefree chatter and glitter of the occasion – all are skilfully suggested at the start by Berlioz's adroit scoring, which includes four harps (the first time the harp had been used in a symphony). The waltz begins, gracefully and with a feeling of total ease and decorum. The artist takes a partner and joins in, lost for a moment in the magic of the dance.

All at once his heart sinks. There, across the hall, he espies his unobtainable beloved. She rises to take the floor with another. How smoothly she moves! How gracefully she dances! Then she is lost in the swirl of dancers and the artist must show to his present partner an attentiveness he does not feel.

At length the waltz builds to its climax, but its rush is arrested for the artist by the persistent thought of his beloved, and the end of the dance is ruined for him. It turns into a frenetic scurry and ends in a jagged chord.

Third movement: Adagio

Scene in the country. Alone in the country on a summer's evening, the artist hears two distant herdsmen calling to each other in a ranz des vaches *(an alphorn melody of the Swiss Alps). Their pastoral duet, the rustle of wind in the trees, and the hope that his beloved might yet be his, all lull him into a reverie, but the* idée fixe *returns in his dreams. His heart palpitates and he experiences dread premonitions. The sun sets, there is thunder in the distance, then solitude and silence.*

For his two Swiss 'alphorn' players, Berlioz chose a cor anglais and an oboe. The lonely call of the cor anglais is echoed from a distance by the oboe, and the two spend a leisurely few moments serenading one another, gradually developing the cor anglais's opening idea. The artist dozes. A melody emerges on violins and flute. His sleep becomes increasingly disturbed as the theme is repeated against solemn horn calls and eventually builds into a noble statement. Under an insistent violin figure, the *idée fixe* is heard again on cellos and violas while the song of the quail on woodwind and horn re-establishes the pastoral atmosphere.

Suddenly roused by his reveries, the artist quickly drifts off again, only to be disturbed by a powerful figure on cellos and basses. The *idée fixe* (oboe and flute) alternates with this menacing figure, and there is an intense climax, at the height of which timpani enter, *fortissimo,* now with wooden-headed sticks, creating a harsh effect. A clarinet melody over pizzicato violins brings relative peace to the scene, but soon angry rhythms on lower strings force another moment of frustrated desire, and a return to the *idée fixe* – and to distant thunder. As the sky darkens, the first herdsman (cor anglais) calls again across the valley, but for answer he receives only the sound of threatening thunder (four timpani, played with sponge-headed sticks). Six times he calls, but, eventually realizing that the elements are to be his only reply, he makes his sad way home.

Berlioz spares us a musical description of the next stage of the story – involving drug-induced trance and murder – for he has even more frightful horrors in store.

Fourth movement: Allegretto non troppo

March to the guillotine. In despair the artist attempts to commit suicide by taking an overdose of opium, but the drug, too weak to prove fatal, instead induces fearsome dreams. He dreams that he has killed his beloved, is condemned to death, and is being taken for execution.

The third movement takes us into the country (below) where the artist, alone in the fields, is lulled into a reverie by the distant calls of herdsmen and the rustle of wind in the trees, only to be disturbed by a dream of his beloved.

The idée fixe *floats into his mind, only to be terminated by the fall of the blade.*

This grotesque march was rescued by the composer from an unsuccessful opera and is, again, a symphonic novelty. Timpani, at first struck with sponge, then with wooden sticks, take an important role, contributing to the nightmare aspect of the gruesome ceremony. Two cornets are called for, and two ophicleides (named from the greek ophis + kleides = 'keyed serpent', a bass wind instrument made of brass. Because of its extraordinary tone it was once nicknamed 'chromatic bullock') which today are usually replaced by tubas.

Drums commence the march. They are answered by a syncopated horn rhythm that stretches mournfully as it progresses. There is a rapid timpani crescendo, and the drooping melody of the march appears. On its second appearance there is an irreverent countertheme on bassoon. Then come the drums again, inexorable, diabolically jubilant. Violins take up the march theme, punctuated by a jagged chord on woodwind and brass, *fortissimo.* Bassoons enter again with a chattering theme over pizzicato strings, but they are swallowed up in the second theme of the march – a typically French melody that

has something in common with the *Marseillaise,* so often heard in the revolutionary times that led up to the first performance of the *Symphonie Fantastique.*

After the repeat of this entire first section, the French march is continued through the middle section with the lead taken by blaring brass accompanied by ever more elaborate and feverish contributions from the other instruments, especially the drums. With a hideous jeering laugh, woodwind and middle strings reintroduce the drooping march theme, now driven forward by bizarre embellishments. At one point it is turned upside-down. The whole grisly assembly joins in the final terrifying statement, bass drum and cymbals marking the off-beats, brass, woodwind and timpani emphasizing the rhythm, and strings playing the part of the exultant crowd thirsting for blood.

An instant of quiet as the victim mounts the steps, and the crowd roars its delight. The neck is laid on the slot and the watchers hold their breath. On solo clarinet the *idée fixe* passes through the terrified artist's head; then his head is severed from his body (*fortissimo* chord) and bounces into the basket (*pizzicato* strings). Cheers from the satisfied rabble.

Fifth movement: Larghetto-allegro-allegro assai

Dream of a Witches' Sabbath. The artist at a Witches' Sabbath hears again the idée fixe, *but now transformed into a brazen and trivial dance. She has come to witness his burial! Later comes a monstrous parody of the* Dies Irae *('Day of Wrath', from the Latin* Mass for the Dead*). The dance of the witches is combined with the* Dies Irae.

The composer's drugged nightmare transcends even the guillotine. Weird, half-formed shapes meet him, and an echo of the jeering laugh heard in the march is his only welcome to a scene of darkness and demons. An ugly cackle is heard on flutes and oboe. It is perhaps a recollection of the very first notes of the symphony, as if the artist, looking back, regrets in vain ever having set out on his adventure. It is echoed by muted horn over a menacing roll on the bass drum. These creepy effects – the weird shapes, the laugh, and the cackles – pass before the artist once more as if in some inescapable and malevolent

The terrifying final movement is vividly evoked by Goya's painting of a Witches' Sabbath. *Here, the witches, their forms hideously misshapen and distorted by degradation, wait with gleeful anticipation to be presented to the Devil.*

circular cortège. Then comes the most chilling figure of all: the *idée fixe* enters on solo clarinet in a gawky and distorted dance accompanied only by two timpani. The beloved herself is present amongst the witches and prepares to lead them in a dance:

Example 3

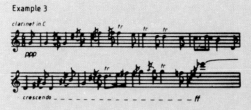

At that last high note the whole gathering of demons and witches screams its approval, then moves in close to prepare for the orgy. Again the *idée fixe* is heard, this time on a clarinet in E flat, an instrument of piercing and unlovely tone, and accompanied now by other harsh woodwind, with four bassoons adding rapid ascending phrases, like bubbles rising in a boiling cauldron. In no time at all the whole company is whirling in abandoned glee, but with a judder the dance is arrested and a dramatic passage on bassoons, cellos and double basses drags the proceedings to the lower regions.

Baleful funeral bells sound in the distance, calling for solemnity. The dancers twice attempt to restart their cavorting, only to be crushed by savage chords. As the bells continue their mournful tolling, the *Dies Irae* sounds out on two bassoons and two tubas at a deliberate pace. This is repeated at twice the speed by horns and trombones, and then again, faster still and with scant reverence, by high woodwind and pizzicato strings to represent the acclamation of the dancers. They end their version with a hideous shriek. A variation of the *Dies Irae* is given the same three-fold treatment; then again, like some dread dictum that will not be denied, the original version is thrice-repeated in the same terms.

But the dancers' energy will not be denied. Amid stern warnings from brass, they begin again their convulsive dance. To convey the confused aspect of the scene as various groups prance about, Berlioz constructs a *fugue* (in which the subject is given out by one section of the orchestra and 'answered' by another), against which the warning brass chords, disorientated by the throng, stab through like forked tongues. It was such effects as these that caused critics of the day to complain that Berlioz 'invents new rhythms.' Even if this were true, it is hardly

a crime. The eerie dance runs its length until the brass warnings gather themselves for a renewed attack and the dance disintegrates, the woodwind crying out in drooping two-note phrases. Two horns utter an invitation to continue the dance. It is accepted spasmodically by bassoons and lower strings, but they become intertwined with the *Dies Irae* before building in strength and terror over a crescendo bass drum roll.

At last the *Dies Irae,* on oboes, clarinets, bassoons, horns, cornets, trombones and tuba, and the dance on strings, piccolo and flute, combine in an amazing sequence of deliberation and abandon. The tension is raised still further by the violins in an ascending repetition of the disorientated brass chords; then, perhaps to imitate the dry rattle of dancing skeletons, the violins and violas reverse their bows and play a rhythm on their strings with the wood. Over this, woodwind continue the dance, but they are suddenly left alone and quickly tumble into chaos. Orchestral chords round them up, and they squeal their acknowledgement. Disruptive rhythms now take charge: the *Dies Irae,* its three diminishing statements telescoped together, now precipitates a final hectic climax. The soul of the doomed artist is claimed by a triumphant Satan.

Great interpreters

Sir Colin Davis (conductor)

Sir Colin Davis has had a passion for the work of Berlioz since the very beginning of his career as a conductor and composer. With the London Symphony Orchestra he embarked upon the recording of all Berlioz's most important scores. It is very much due to his dedication and diligence that so many of Berlioz's finest works are now available in recorded form. An almost uncanny empathy between composer and conductor has been commented on when Davis and the LSO perform the *Symphonie Fantastique* or other major works — as though the spirit of Berlioz lived again in all its sometimes macabre genius, inspiring the orchestra. Sir Colin is also associated with the music of Mozart and Tippett.

FURTHER LISTENING

Harold in Italy, op. 16 (1834)
With *Harold in Italy,* a self-styled 'programmatic' symphony with viola *obbligato* (a part that must *always* be played), Berlioz reached a watershed in his career. In it a new sense of balance and serenity is seen emerging after the intoxication of the *Symphonie Fantastique;* only the last movement, the 'Orgy of the Brigands', shows the extravagances of old.

Nuits d'Eté, op. 7 (1834–41)
In this charming song-cycle, Berlioz composed some of his most refreshingly melodic and beautiful music. The cycle was originally scored for voice and piano, but its true nature was only revealed by the composer's later orchestration of all six songs. The voice is constantly underpinned and supported by lush, transparent orchestral settings. The warmth of long summer nights floods through each piece.

La Damnation de Faust, op. 24 (1846)
The *Damnation* displays Berlioz's unique musical conception in his decision to adapt Goethe's story to the old Cantata format (a lyrical piece for solo voices, chorus and orchestra) rather than an operatic one. That done, none of the dramatic impact of the tale is lost, and the orchestra is free to deliver some telling music within the connecting material between each 'scene'. At the same time, the choir and soloists carry the tale forward with absolutely no lapse in pace.

'A *wonderful spectacle*'

*Berlioz, who cast his professional eye over the musical
instrument section, was one of the millions who
visited the Great Exhibition – Britain's triumphant
celebration of her industrial achievements.*

There had been exhibitions before in the world, but London's Great Exhibition of 1851 outclassed them all and inspired all others. Approximately 112,000 items from all parts of the world were housed in one of the wonders of the age – Joseph Paxton's Crystal Palace – and more than six million people, including many foreign visitors, came to see it. For that year nobody could talk of anything else and for a whole generation the event was continually recalled with wonder.

The Exhibition of the Works of Industry of all Nations opened on the first of May amid scenes of great pomp and tremendous popular enthusiasm. This was just two years after the Prince Consort, Albert, had summoned a small organizing committee to discuss his scheme for an international show to celebrate peace, prosperity and progress. The committee responded well, and so did Britain's leading manufacturers and representatives of the colonies and of the great foreign nations. The government sanctioned the use of a site in the prestigiously central Hyde Park and 254 designs and specifications for exhibition buildings flooded in to the committee. But it was Albert, whose brainchild the whole scheme was, who picked Joseph Paxton's design.

Paxton's Palace

In doing so Albert picked a winner. Joseph Paxton himself was a personality as new and typical of his age as his building. It was very fitting that a man who had risen from being, in Queen Victoria's words, 'a common gardener's boy' should have supplied the design rather than one of the professional architects who had also competed. As the Duke of Devonshire's head gardener at Chatsworth, Paxton had designed fabulous conservatories and the Crystal Palace was basically an enormous conservatory of glass and iron, a hugely magnified version of Chatsworth's Lily House. It covered 19 acres and the transepts were 108 feet high so as to accommodate some of the loftiest elms growing in Hyde Park.

Once his design had been selected, Paxton's 'showy bauble' went up in a remarkably short time, even by modern standards. It was erected in only five months by novel mass-production and prefabrication methods. All of its ingredients were interchangeable: the girders, columns, gutters and sash bars were identical throughout. The glass, a material newly freed from a heavy tax, glittered and sparkled in its parkland setting, and the whole effect was as magical as it was practical. 'We shall be disappointed,' *Punch* told its readers, 'if the next generation of London children are not brought up like cucumbers under glass.' So far so good for Prince Albert's vision, but as the opening day approached old and new objections were raised.

Many influential people and politicians, such as the Duke of Wellington and Disraeli, were cynical about Albert's 'raree-show' or only pragmatically supportive – it would distract people from the government's difficulties. But others were downright hostile. It was suggested that the Exhibition would bring down the wrath of God upon its vainglorious perpetrators and that it would act as a magnet for all the ruffians and subversives of Britain and Europe. Important foreign visitors, not to mention the royal family, would risk their lives in attending the opening, a day that would surely see riot and revolution. Technical objections were also voiced. The palace had been built over existing trees, so it was feared that sparrows' droppings would annihilate every person and object beneath, while the sounding of the royal salute at the Queen's entrance would shatter the glass and make

Christened the 'Crystal Palace' by a writer in Punch *magazine, Paxton's exhibition building (left) was an unqualified success – 'a more fitting temple for the world's industrial treasures could not be devised.' There were anxieties about the safety of this revolutionary building, so a section of the interior wooden galleries was built on the ground and 'tested' by having workmen jump on it and soldiers march over it.*

24

mincemeat of all the assembled dignitaries. But the show went on despite the scaremongering: how could the Queen refuse to open her beloved husband's most ambitious project?

A day to live for ever

In fact Victoria performed her official duties in a positive trance of joy. She was genuinely favourable towards all she saw and probably a very good gauge of popular taste. Her own description of the opening ceremony cannot be bettered:

The Park presented a wonderful spectacle, crowds streaming through it – carriages and troops passing, quite like the Coronation and for me the same anxiety . . . The Green Park and Hyde Park were one mass of densely crowded human beings, in the highest good humour and most enthusiastic . . . the sun shone and gleamed upon the gigantic edifice, upon which the flags of every nation were flying. We drove up Rotten Row and got out of our carriages at the entrance on that side. The glimpse through the iron gates of the transept, the waving palms and flowers, the myriads of people filling the galleries and seats around, together with the flourish of trumpets as we entered the building, gave a sensation I shall never forget and I felt much moved . . . The sight as we came to the centre where the steps and chair (on which I did not sit) was placed facing the beautiful crystal fountain was magic and impressive. The tremendous cheering, the joy expressed in every face, the vastness of the building, with all its decoration and exhibits, the sound of the organ (with 200 instruments and 600 voices which yet seemed nothing) and my beloved husband, the creator of this peace festival 'uniting the industry and art of all nations', all this was indeed moving, and a day to live for ever.

A striking incident occurred just after the Archbishop of Canterbury had delivered a short prayer and the choir had burst into the *Hallelujah Chorus*. At that moment a Chinese man dressed in full national costume stepped out into the middle of the central nave and, advancing slowly towards the royal group, did obeisance to her majesty. Victoria was deeply impressed and so sure that her admirer was an eminent mandarin – there were, after all, no other representatives from China present – that she

requested that he be included in the diplomatic cortege. Accordingly, and with the utmost gravity, the splendidly robed Chinaman followed immediately behind the ambassadors in the final procession. But he was never seen again and an unkind rumour circulated to the effect that he had been a very convincing imposter from a junk moored on the Thames.

But Victoria was not the only person to wax lyrical about the proceedings. In a less bubbly vein the *Times* echoed her sentiments so precisely that Victoria cherished this clipping:

There was yesterday witnessed a sight the like of which has never happened before, and which, in the nature of things, can never be repeated . . . In a building that could easily have accommodated twice as many, twenty-five thousand persons, so it is computed, were arranged in order around the throne of our SOVEREIGN. Around them, amidst them, and over their heads was displayed all that is useful or beautiful in nature or in art. Above them rose a glittering arch far more lofty and spacious than the vaults of even our noblest cathedrals. On either side the vista seemed almost boundless . . . Some saw in it the second and more glorious inauguration of their SOVEREIGN; some a solemn dedication of art and its stores; some were most reminded of that day when all ages and climes shall be gathered around the throne of their Maker.

The 'marriage of industry and art'

On the opening day many of the foreign exhibits lay wrapped and undisplayed in the side aisles, and because the Baltic ports had been late in thawing, the Russian exhibits were not in place until the end of May. But since the Exhibition contained far more than could be digested in a dozen visits, let alone a single day, these initial hitches went unnoticed. The Exhibition was resolutely international in its scope. Britain's manufacturers had been sure enough in their industrial supremacy to desire 'a clear stage and no favour'. But that supremacy was reflected in the fact that one half of the total exhibition space was occupied by Great Britain and the colonies, with the other half being allocated to the foreign exhibitors, of which France and Germany were the most important. The huge task of classifying the exhibits had fallen upon a rising young scientist and public servant, Lyon Playfair (by name and by nature!). He devised four

Henry Selous's official painting of the opening ceremony (left). The Queen, Prince Albert and their eldest children (the future Edward VII is wearing a kilt) are on the dais, which is overlooked by members of the public in the galleries. Exhibition Commissioners, court officials and important foreign visitors are gathered in the foreground. The mysterious Chinese emissary is at the right of the picture.

An Overland Journey to the Great Exhibition, showing a few extra articles and visitors. *Artist Richard Doyle's playful fantasy (far left) reveals the contemporary feeling that the whole world and its goods were coming to London for the Great Exhibition.*

The Eastern, or Foreign, Nave of the Crystal Palace, photographed by the Calotype process when the Exhibition was closed. The large sack-like shape in front is the top of a trophy made of vulcanized rubber objects. Behind this is Professor Kiss's 'stupendous conception', a sculpture of a lioness attacking an Amazon on horseback, while blocking the view is a display of glass from Milan.

main categories for them: Raw Materials (ranging from the biggest lump of coal ever mined intact to a bundle of peacock feathers), Machinery, Manufacturers and Fine Arts. There was also a miscellaneous section, which accommodated many of the more ludicrous items submitted.

The Exhibition's promoters were most infatuated with 'self-acting machinery' and the technological miracles it might perform, and the Machinery Court was the most crowded area in the Palace. Here besmocked farmers gathered excitedly around the reaping machine from America, while mechanics down from the north and Birmingham clustered around the Jacquard loom. The Queen, a frequent visitor, was impressed with a medal-making machine that was capable of producing 50 million medals a week and she was also enraptured with the electric telegraph by means of which she despatched messages to her loyal subjects in Scotland.

Despite this understandable preoccupation with all that was most modern and mechanical, the Exhibition was faithful to Albert's interest in uniting all the arts, industrial, handicraft and fine. Thus Sèvres pottery and exquisite Spanish lace were prominently displayed, and a good deal of space was devoted to needlework. But in many ways the Exhibition honoured handicraft unconsciously, for at this stage in the industrial revolution very little was genuinely machine-made. The Crystal Palace itself enshrined this duality in that, though the mahogany for the galleries had been turned with the aid of steam power, the 300,000 panes of glass had been blown by hand. Industrial materials such as iron and steel did not always mean 'industrial' processes. The displays of Sheffield cutlery and edge tools excited great attention and admiration among foreign visitors (the Sheffield Court was one of the most extensive in the building), while domestic

visitors were, it seems, unusually absorbed by the impenetrable locks, 'myriad permutation' keys and incombustible safes of the craftsmanlike Messrs Chubb, Bramah & Mordan.

There was something for everyone, especially for the newly prosperous Victorian middle class, who formed the bulk of the visitors. The bulging, opulent household items on display were the epitome of Victorian 'kitsch' but very pleasing to consumers who loved combinations of new technology with lavish ornamentation. Even so, some must have baulked at the enormous Tudor-style sideboard made entirely out of rubber. Indeed the Exhibition was often as entertaining as it was informative. Many of the miscellaneous exhibits were as hilariously grotesque as they were ingenious. There was, for example, a pair of cuffs hand-spun and hand-knitted from the wool of French poodle dogs, and what could have been more inspiring than the curious 'Anaxyridian trousers', a garment which, according to the *Official Catalogue,* were so shaped that 'they remain as a fixture to the heel without straps and dispense with braces'. Who could forget the amazing 'cricket catapult', a device 'for propelling the ball in the absence of a first-rate bowler'?

Much of the Exhibition's success must have been due to the fact that it operated on many levels. Some exhibits could even be titillating. In the sculpture sections of Fine Arts, for example, Hiram Power's 'Greek Slave' was immensely popular. Female nudes were a tolerable object of mass observation if there was a moral involved and here was 'a young and beautiful Greek girl, deprived of her clothing and exposed for sale to some wealthy eastern barbarian, before whom she is supposed to stand, with an expression of mournful dejection mingled with shame and disgust.' From industrial machines and examples of medieval armour to huge ecclesiastical ornaments, no one was disappointed. Even without the exhibits, or the festive atmosphere always generated by large crowds, the Crystal Palace in itself was deemed well worth a visit. Its centrepiece, the crystal fountain, which glittered 'in all the colours of the rainbow' was one of the Exhibition's chief 'attractions'.

The Great Exhibition was a genuinely popular event. The *Times* had marvelled at the 25,000 persons present at the opening ceremony, but the Palace proved capable of accommodating twice that number at a time without seeming too crowded. During the 141 days of the Exhibition (it was closed on Sundays although Sabbath-maintaining vigilantes were still upset by the fact that some exhibits had been photographed on the Lord's Day) it never failed to draw the crowds. The average daily attendance was 42,831 and the greatest number of people admitted on any one day (7 October) was 109,915.

The 'pounds' and the 'shillings'

The organizers' democratic policy on admission prices led to a curious demarcation between the 'pounds' and the 'shillings'. Season tickets started out expensively enough at three guineas for men and two guineas for women, but after 31 July they were considerably reduced. By the end of May daily admission fees of a shilling from Monday to Thursday, half a crown for Friday and five shillings for Saturday were in operation.

These prices enabled the respectable 'lower orders' to attend, as befitted the organizers' interest in celebrating the 'working bees of the world's hive' as much as 'captains of industry'. Also, cheap train excursions (in the provision of which Thomas Cook was involved) helped to make the event a truly national as well as an international one. Most

New ploughs, improved carts, mechanical threshers and steam-operated machines filled up the farming section (above left), while the strangely named 'hardware' area boasted many of the less utilitarian and grossly ornate household items that were so dear to the Victorians (above).

Though the Great Exhibition was the celebration of the 1850s, it failed in one respect to impress its visitors – the refreshments were a scandal. There were sandwiches that were alleged to be the 'worst and smallest' ever tasted and very expensive and dry 'dollops of pork pie'.

BBC Hulton Picture Library

BBC Hulton Picture Library

This selection of objects demonstrates the extraordinary, sometimes comical diversity of the exhibits. Thus the latest in fancy tableware vied with the 'preserved pig', 'cured entire' by a Dublin provision merchant, Kean's travelling bedstead and the typical ornate Royal Albert skate, 'decidedly the handsomest skate ever manufactured'.

remarkably, given the prejudices and phobias of the scaremongerers, the 'pounds' and 'shillings' mingled without incident. At all times the crowds were orderly and quiet and there wasn't a single serious accident (some French crockery got broken on 7 October). This says much for the effectiveness of Paxton's design, for the intrinsic appeal of the Exhibition and perhaps for the good sense of its organizers in banning the sale of alcohol as well as smoking. It was all thoroughly respectable. Women could attend unaccompanied without risk to their reputations, and that was an achievement in Victorian London.

Amidst the general approval, however, there was one consistent complaint: nobody had a good word to say about the catering arrangements, which quickly acquired the status that junk-food catering has today. Although 1,092,337 bottles of soft drinks were sold, together with 943,691 Bath buns and 870,027 plain ones, as well as a variety of other 'eatables', the

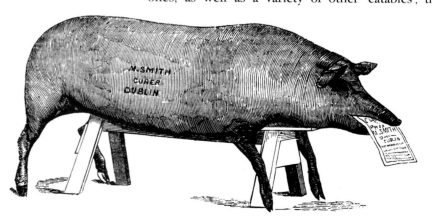

punters were unhappy. The food was described as outrageously expensive and poor in quality. It was, moreover, served by slovenly and inattentive young women. One letter-writer to the *Morning Chronicle* had this to say about the situation:

Pray assist to remedy a most universal complaint of all those hungry curious at the Great Exhibition, by giving the young females at the refreshment tables a hint that their personal appearances, as well as their hands and faces, would be greatly improved by a moderate use of soap. The excuse of not having had time since the 1st of May to wash themselves certainly appears true, but the contractor would do well, in case of increasing business, to have relays of washed damsels if he wishes to see his eatables well digested.

Catering apart, the Exhibition was a resounding commercial and social success. Although Colonel Sibthorp, one of the project's bitterest and most bigoted critics from the beginning, still railed against 'a palace of tomfoolery, stuffed with foreign rubbish' in which the poor had been cheated of their dearly-earned pittances, most of the critics were silenced and many joined in the chorus of praise. Congratulations from public bodies poured in; the City of Paris gave a great fête to the Exhibition committee; and Victoria and Albert made a triumphant tour of the north of England. The staggering profit of £186,437 was used for the nation's long-term benefit in that it purchased land in South Kensington for the erection of a permanent national museum – the Victoria and Albert Museum – as well as funding research grants and scholarships, and handsomely rewarding such crucially important individuals as Joseph Paxton, who was awarded a bursary of £5,000.

The Exhibition was also successful as a gigantic public relations stunt for industrial Britain in its heyday, and it incidentally facilitated the development of the important new industry of tourism in that every other attraction in London boomed as a result. But far from marking the ongoing triumph of Britain as the foremost industrial economy of the world, it marked the beginning of the end. It is an ironic fact that the exhibits entered by the United States, apart from the celebrated McCormick reaping machine, were not considered to be impressive. The Americans had laid claim to far more space than they proved able to fill and the huge sculpture of an American eagle that surmounted their section aroused snide comments on the USA as a boastful, upstart nation too big for its boots. By the 1870s, however, the tables had turned. The USA and Germany took the industrial lead and though Britain's relegation to a second place was more than compensated for economically by the acquisition of an enormous empire, the Great Exhibition of 1851

BBC Hulton Picture Library

The title page from sheet music (above right) commemorating the gathering of nations occasioned by the Exhibition.

The Crammond Collection

Prince Albert presided over the closing of the Exhibition on 15 October in the absence of the Queen, who was 'grieved' at being unable to attend. In contrast with the opening ceremony it was a sombre and solemn affair, and, appropriately enough, it was a very wet day.

had marked the true but nonetheless temporary mid-Victorian climax.

In the sphere of international understanding and peace Albert's vision was frustrated. He had hoped that the Exhibition would serve as 'a new starting point, from which all nations will be able to direct their future exertions' but within a few years the Crimean War had broken out. There was also a certain grim significance, which went unperceived at the time, in the award of one of the Exhibition prizes to Krupps of Essen in Germany for a gun made of superior quality cast steel.

More than any exhibit, or any of the rhetoric, the element that made the Great Exhibition endure as a profoundly important event was the Crystal Palace. By September visitors were being rung out of the building well before six o'clock because of the inadequacy of the gaslight installed, and 11 October was the last day of the Exhibition. Many of the exhibits were sold; some were presented to Queen Victoria; some were left in the Park either because they were too bulky to move, or because no one wanted to buy them; and some found a home in the Victoria and Albert Museum.

It was now time to dismantle the Palace as scheduled. But the building had been so popular, and so readily accepted as a new landmark, that many people were reluctant to see it come down. There was a brief campaign to keep it, with suggestions that it should be turned into a Winter Garden and various other schemes, but after a debate in Parliament, it was decided to go ahead with the original plan to dismantle the Palace. Eventually, Paxton himself

formed a new company, which bought the component parts from the contractors who had built the Palace and arranged for its migration to Sydenham in south London. There it was the scene of exhibitions and concerts, as well as an important social centre for Londoners, until fire destroyed it for ever in 1936.

Before the move was underway thousands of people continued to visit the empty Palace and sometimes military bands gave concerts there until the summer of 1852. Victoria was particularly wistful about the ending of the Exhibition and now the forlorn Palace, which had, after all, represented the climax of her husband's career. She took the whole event very personally, even noting in her journal that the final day was the 12th anniversary of her betrothal to Albert – 'a curious coincidence'. After her last visit to the Palace Victoria wrote:

I could not believe it was the last time I was to see it. An organ, accompanied by a fine and powerful wind instrument called the sommerphone, was being played, and it nearly upset me. The canvas is very dirty, the red curtains are faded and many things are very much soiled, still the effect is fresh and new as ever and most beautiful. The glass fountain . . . was already removed . . . and the sappers and miners were rolling about the little boxes just as they did at the beginning. It made us all very melancholy.

In fact it was not the last time Victoria visited the Crystal Palace, for when it re-opened in Sydenham in 1854 she presided over the ceremony. This time, however, no opportune 'mandarin' came forward to add a certain glamour to the scene.

THE GREAT COMPOSERS

Felix Mendelssohn

1809-1847

Felix Mendelssohn is considered to have been one of the foremost composers of the early 19th-century Romantic movement. He was loved both in his native country of Germany and abroad, especially in Britain. Because of his popularity, Mendelssohn travelled widely and, as the Listener's Guide describes, much of his loveliest music was composed as a direct result of the inspiration he gained in countries as diverse as Scotland and Italy. One of Mendelssohn's most frequent destinations was Britain, where Queen Victoria and her consort, Prince Albert, were two of his most fervent admirers. In the Background examines the complex woman who gave her name to the age, as well as one of the most salient features of 19th-century Europe: the extension of basic education from the upper and middle classes to the general population.

Composer's life

Unlike other 19th-century Romantic composers, Mendelssohn did not outwardly have to struggle and suffer for his art. Handsome, charming, debonair and, above all, the 'perfect gentleman', Mendelssohn was immediately accepted by his upper- and middle-class admirers. He was born into a well-to-do family that encouraged his talents: as well as being a considerable musical prodigy, he showed a talent for painting, drawing and literature. This material comfort has led critics to undervalue Mendelssohn's musical achievements. However, although his background circumstances were easy, Mendelssohn did not have a comfortable life: he did not compose easily, constantly feeling the need to revise his works; his professional relationships were not easy – he always felt aggrieved at not being appointed as conductor of the Singakademie in Berlin; and his close relationship with his sister Fanny was expressed in language dramatic enough for the most extreme Romantic.

COMPOSER'S LIFE
'A most amiable man'

A child prodigy, remarkable for his depth and sensitivity as well as his precocity, Mendelssohn flowered into one of the most celebrated – and best-loved – composers of his time.

Felix Mendelssohn does not conform to the popular idea of a struggling Romantic composer. He did not write by the guttering flame of a candle in an unheated garret or die, unrecognized, in poverty. He was born into a wealthy and cultured family who did all they could to encourage his prodigious musical talents. By the age of nine he was an acclaimed performer; at 16 he had proved his genius as a composer. Artist, poet, traveller and even mountaineer, he was a man of great sensitivity and charm who numbered among his friends the great and famous and the literary and musical giants of his day.

As a young boy he won the heart of Goethe; in his prime he captivated Queen Victoria. When he died – at only 37 – two nations went into mourning, for the composer, and the man. Although Mendelssohn had much music still to give, he had already laid the cornerstone for modern musical appreciation in the Western world.

A cultured background
The influence of Mendelssohn's family on his life and works start with his grandfather, Moses Mendelssohn. Born in Dessau, into poverty and under the severe restrictions imposed on Jews by 18th-century Prussia, Moses took his destiny into his own hands. At the age of 14 he walked 80 miles to Berlin, where he taught himself languages, mathematics and philosophy. He became one of the great thinkers and teachers of the Enlightenment period and his writings were translated into 30 languages. He was a champion of religious tolerance and fought in particular for Jewish emancipation. Both his philosophical ideals and his talent for making money were passed on to his son Abraham, who became a banker and married the musical and highly-educated Lea Salomon.

The young couple settled in Hamburg, where their eldest child, Mendelssohn's beloved sister, Fanny, was born in 1805. Lea noted with uncanny foresight that the baby had 'Bach fugue fingers' – and indeed, had the convention of the time allowed, there is little doubt that Fanny would have become a composer of distinction. As it was, she contented herself with writing songs and performing recitals of other people's music. The composer of the family was to be Felix, born in February, 1809. He was followed by two more children, Rebekka and Paul.

Two years after Felix was born, the family uprooted. Abraham, like many other bankers and merchants of Hamburg, had managed to dodge Napoleon's trade restrictions and had become very rich indeed. Like them, he was now faced with a more direct threat from the occupying French troops. The Mendelssohns fled to Berlin.

Mendelssohn at 20, newly arrived in London. Charming, gracious and debonair, he immediately won the hearts of the English. They were not only moved by the warmth and sentiment of his music, but also found him to be the perfect gentleman.

Bildarchiv Preussischer Kulturbesitz

The happy, comfortable and enlightened environment in which the young Mendelssohn grew up was made possible by the courage and determination of his grandfather, Moses (right). As a boy, Moses, a poor hunchback Jew, had walked the 80 miles to Berlin, in the hope of making a better life for himself. There, against a background of prejudice, he prospered, winning a name for himself as a philosopher and champion of Jewish emancipation.

Mendelssohn at 12 (below) – a brilliant child who captivated everyone he met.

In Berlin, Abraham made a significant contribution to the defence of Prussia by equipping voluntary soldiers and financing a military hospital. After the victory over Napoleon he was rewarded with a position on Berlin's Municipal Council and an elevated status not usually accorded to a Jew. Partly out of Christian conviction and partly to cement their new standing, the family added the name Bartholdy, which had been adopted by Abraham's brother, to their own.

Musical beginnings

In this illustrious setting, the young boy's genius took root and flourished. He was given a rounded education under Berlin's most prestigious teachers. His principal music tutor was Carl Zelter, a colourful man whose coarse behaviour and unconventional dress were more suited to his previous occupation as a stonemason than to his post as the Director of Berlin's Singakademie.

Zelter's pupil went from strength to strength. At nine he was performing, as a pianist or conductor, before an admiring circle of family and friends – including some of Germany's foremost writers, poets and philosophers – Heine, Hegel, Humboldt and Jakob Grimm were among those who heard him play. At ten Felix began to compose; a young friend witnessed the scene:

I found him on a footstool, before a small table, writing with such earnestness. On my asking what he was about, he replied, gravely, 'I am finishing my new Quartet for piano and stringed instruments.'... looking over his shoulder [I] saw as beautiful a score as if it had been written by the most skilled copyist. It was his first Quartet in C minor. Then, forgetting quartets, ... down we went into the garden, he clearing high hedges with a leap, running, singing and climbing trees like a squirrel.

The boy's energy amazed all who knew him. He studied; he composed without ceasing; at the age of 12 he even started his own newspaper. His mother, with her usual intuition, wrote that 'his impulsiveness sometimes makes him work harder than he ought to at his age.' Mendelssohn would always work harder than he ought to – and one day it would kill him.

At the age of 12 Zelter's protégé so impressed him that he proposed to introduce him to Goethe, scientist, sage, poet, and Germany's foremost philosopher and thinker. When Goethe agreed to see him, his family were thrown into a state of excitement, but Felix was not overawed and reported in a letter home:

He was in the garden and just coming round a hedge. He is very friendly, but I don't think any of the pictures are like him. One would never take him for 73 but 50.

And later he told of their daily routine:

I play here much more than I do at home: rarely less than four hours, sometimes six or even eight. Goethe sits down beside me and when I have finished ... I ask for a kiss or take one. You cannot imagine how good and kind he is to me.

It was the beginning of a friendship that was to last until Goethe's death and spanned five significant visits. The relationship deepened Mendelssohn's love for classical literature, and assured its importance in the composition of his music. For his part, Goethe was not only entertained and amused by his young companion, but prompted to a greater appreciation of classical music, though he never managed to share Mendelssohn's enthusiasm for Beethoven.

After the visit to Goethe the family, with its entourage of tutors, embarked on a tour of Switzerland. Felix absorbed each new impression voraciously; once awakened, his passion for travelling would never die. As on later journeys, he sketched or painted views that struck him with their beauty, and wrote copious letters and poems, often illustrating them with amusing cartoons. He also commented on the native taste in music – yodelling:

This kind of singing sounds harsh and unpleasant when it is heard nearby, or in a room . . . in the valleys, mountains and woods, when you hear it mingling with the answering echoes, it sounds beautiful.

This is early evidence of the critical awareness of the music of others that made him determined to bring good music to the people – to teach musicians to play and the public to listen – which was to be one of his major achievements.

Germany's new composer

Meanwhile, the budding composer delighted his teacher with a one-act opera, *The Uncle from Boston*. After its performance Zelter addressed the audience

Archiv für Kunst und Geschichte

Carl Zelter (left) was an inspired choice as Mendelssohn's music teacher. Something of a rough diamond, he was renowned for his lack of tact, and could be relied upon to lower the tone of conversation. Yet, despite his boorishness, Zelter was a man of utter integrity, and, in Goethe's words, one of 'subtle and diamantine genius'.

Mendelssohn, the child prodigy, plays before the illustrious Goethe at one of the regular Sunday morning musical parties organized by his family (below). The young boy was to strike up a surprisingly close friendship with the 73-year-old writer and philosopher – then struggling to complete part II of Faust.

Archiv für Kunst und Geschichte

In addition to his many talents – composer, poet and even mountaineer – Mendelssohn was also an artist of some ability. He painted this charming view of Lucerne (above) while on a trip to Switzerland, inspired by the serenity of the landscape.

One of Mendelssohn's greatest triumphs was his rediscovery and revival of Bach's St Matthew Passion (right). Prior to this Bach had been regarded by the public as 'a powdered wig stuffed with learning.' Now Mendelssohn created a whole new wave of interest in the Baroque composer. 'To think', he exclaimed, 'that . . . a Jew should give back to the people the greatest Christian music in the world.'

and congratulated the 14-year-old: 'My dear boy, from this day you are no longer an apprentice, but a full member of the brotherhood of musicians. I hereby proclaim you independent in the name of Mozart, Haydn and old father Bach.'

But Abraham still needed convincing that music was the right career for his son. He took him to Paris to see the composer Cherubini, who was Director of the Paris Conservatoire. The verdict was decisive: 'Your boy is talented, he will do well. He has already done well.' Barely a year later, Cherubini was proved right. At the age of 16, Mendelssohn completed his String Octet, op. 20, which was partly inspired by lines from Goethe's *Faust*. It is recognised as his first fully mature work, and some critics claim it is an unparalleled achievement for a 16-year-old; not even Mozart or Schubert produced music of such brilliance so young. Germany had a new composer.

His next work was another masterpiece, his overture to *A Midsummer Night's Dream*. Again the inspiration came from classical literature, and it has been said that no other music has so successfully captured the essence of Shakespeare. Mendelssohn's friend, the pianist Ignaz Moscheles, declared when he heard it that 'this great and still youthful genius has once again made gigantic steps forward.' Mendelssohn was progressing in other fields too. Having translated Terence's Latin comedy *Andria,* he was awarded a place at the University of Berlin, where he studied aesthetics under the philosopher Hegel.

Mendelssohn next turned his attention to the work

of Johann Sebastian Bach, for many years neglected by the listening public. He spent several years working on the score of *St Matthew Passion,* and when the work was released, it caused a considerable stir in the music world. Tickets for the first performance were sold out within minutes, and some members of the audience were so moved by the music that they wept openly.

Success in Britain

Armed with his now considerable reputation, the 20-year-old set out to conquer more distant lands. He had already made the acquaintance of Sir George Smart, the founder of the Philharmonic Society, and he went to stay in London with the hope of being invited to play there. He was introduced to the pleasures of London life by Moscheles and another friend, Klingemann, both of whom had settled there.

The gaiety and excitement of London after the narrow and stuffy atmosphere of Berlin turned his head and won his heart: it was the beginning of a life-long love affair with England. After three days he wrote home: 'I hardly remember the chief events. Things toss and whirl about me as if I were in a vortex, and I'm whirled along with them. Not in the last six months in Berlin have I seen so many contrasts and such variety as in these three days.' He spent his time driving in Hyde Park, delighting in operas, concerts and balls and the charming young ladies he met there, and marvelling at the thickness of the fog and the even greater density of English plum pudding.

When he made his début, it was to deafening applause and the highest critical acclaim. One reviewer noted 'scarcely had he touched the keyboard than something that can only be described as similar to a pleasurable electric shock passed through his hearers and held them spellbound.' He set the seal on his success and established himself as the darling of the British public with a charity concert for the people of Silesia, who had been made homeless by floods. He was fêted everywhere as a musician of transcendent talent and, no less important to the English, a perfect gentleman.

In July, Mendelssohn and Klingemann travelled to Scotland. The young composer was vividly impressed with the romantic scenery of the Highlands: 'When God himself takes to landscape painting, it turns out strangely beautiful . . . everything looks so stern and robust, half-enveloped in mist or smoke or fog . . .' It inspired him to write his 'Scottish Symphony', and also to take out his drawing pad. During a journey to Fingal's cave, already immortalized a decade earlier by Keats, the first bars of the *Hebrides* Overture occurred to him.

Mendelssohn was less impressed with British folk music. He found the sound of bagpipes offensive to his ear, and when the pair moved on to Wales he wrote: 'Dear me, a harper sits in the hall of every reputed inn, playing incessantly so-called national melodies; that is to say most infamous, vulgar, out-of-tune trash, with a hurdy-gurdy going on at the same time.'

Brotherly love

By the end of August, Mendelssohn was ready to return home. His sister, Fanny, was to be married and he wanted to be at the wedding. But he was prevented from going by a carriage accident that injured his knee. From his sickbed he wrote her a desperate letter.

This then is the last letter you'll receive before your marriage. For the last time I address you as Fräulein Fanny Mendelssohn-Bartholdy . . . There's much I

would like to say to you, but I'm not really able . . . I feel as if I had lost the reins with which formerly I was able to guide my life. When I think about everything which is now going to change, and take a different shape, everything which I have long taken for granted, then my thoughts become unclear and half wild.

The love between brother and sister had always been passionately strong. Felix inevitably showed his compositions to Fanny before anyone else and relied on her advice. In his letters he had addressed her ardently. She made him feel 'quite giddy'. He called her his 'angel', his 'darling little sister' and declared,

In 1829 Mendelssohn travelled to London, where he was immediately plunged into its dazzling social whirl (above). It made Berlin seem positively provincial.

Throughout his life, Mendelssohn shared a deep love and understanding with his sister Fanny (left) – there is no doubt that she was the most important single influence on his life. Their correspondence testifies to the intimacy and, sometimes, intensity of their relationship. When Fanny died – she was suddenly seized by a paralytic stroke while playing the piano – Felix was heartbroken. He collapsed on hearing the news of her death and never fully recovered.

'My sweet, I love you terribly.' On her side, Fanny was no less vehemently attached to her brother. When he left Berlin she wrote 'all will be mute and desolate'. Felix constantly appears in her diary – far more entries are devoted to him than to her fiancé, Wilhelm Hensel. Of him she wrote 'a bridegroom is no more than a man'. Felix's other sister, Rebekka, reported that Fanny fell asleep in Hensel's company – she was bored because he was not there, and on her wedding day she wrote:

I have your portrait before me, and ever repeating your dear name and thinking of you as if you stood at my side, I weep! Every morning and every moment of my life I'll love you from the bottom of my heart, and I'm sure that in doing so I shan't wrong Hensel.

They must have been well aware that the intensity of their love was dangerous. Fanny's marriage was a timely escape. By the time Mendelssohn returned to Berlin for his parents' silver wedding anniversary – having written an operetta for the occasion – she was Frau Hensel.

In 1830 at the age of just 21 Mendelssohn was offered the chair of music at Berlin University, but he refused. He had just begun to compose his 'Reformation' Symphony, and was totally absorbed by it; he wanted to travel; perhaps he also felt it was a mistake to stay too long in the neighbourhood of Fanny and her new husband. His travels were to take him, via a last visit to Goethe, to Austria, Italy, Switzerland and France. He travelled light, taking with him 'three shirts and Goethe's poems'. He met Chopin, Liszt, Berlioz, Paganini, Meyerbeer, Dorothea von Ertmann, who had been a close friend of Beethoven's, and the dramatist Karl Immermann, with whom he intended to collaborate on an opera. His trip to Italy inspired the wonderful 'Italian' Symphony – his Symphony no. 4.

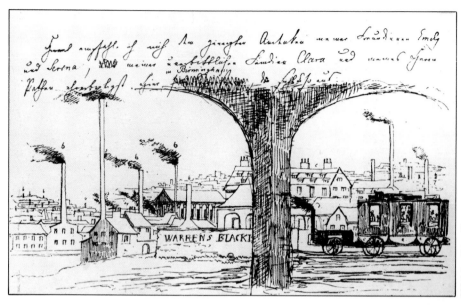

A pen drawing by Mendelssohn of Birmingham (above) where he travelled to conduct the triumphant first performance of his oratorio Elijah *in 1846, just over a year before his death.*

Later achievements
In the spring of 1832, deeply saddened by news of the deaths of Goethe and Zelter, Mendelssohn returned to England. Here his performances drew capacity crowds, but he was called back home by his father, who wanted him to apply for Zelter's post as Director of the Singakademie. In the event he was not disappointed when Zelter's deputy got the job – he had further engagements in London and had been invited to conduct the 1833 Music Festival in Düsseldorf. Here he instituted an important revival of Handel's works besides conducting an impressive series of operas. But neither the audience nor the orchestra lived up to his expectations. He had administrative difficulties and no time for composing. Frustrated beyond endurance, he tore the score of Beethoven's *Egmont* in two during a rehearsal and when, in the summer of 1834, he received an invitation to take over Leipzig's Gewandhaus Orchestra, he accepted with alacrity and relief.

Here in the cultural capital of Germany he had a free hand to organize the city's music and plenty of time in which to compose. During his ten-year stay in Leipzig, he achieved a great deal. He built a first-rate orchestra out of what began as an undistinguished collection of musicians: no doubt they were as encouraged by the enthusiasm of their conductor as by the handsome salary increase he won for them. As usual his repertoire was wide and varied and he introduced the public to works that had hitherto been ignored – including Beethoven's Fourth, and later, his Ninth. He also premièred Schubert's last symphony; Schumann had unearthed the manuscript in Vienna and saved it from almost certain destruction. Another achievement was to invite the leading soloists of the day to perform at the Gewandhaus: all this added up to the tremendous success of his concert seasons, bringing an increased public enthusiasm for music that has formed the basis of all modern musical appreciation.

Short-lived happiness
In 1837 Mendelssohn crowned his happiness by falling in love and getting married. His bride was the

In March, 1837, Mendelssohn married Cécile (above), who bore him five children. The marriage was a very happy one – Cécile was, in Fanny's words, 'a fresh breeze, so bright and natural'.

captivating Cécile Jeanrenaud. It was eight months before Cécile and Fanny met, and Mendelssohn must have been greatly relieved that Fanny found his wife 'a fresh breeze, so bright and natural'. The marriage was a happy one, and there were five children.

In 1840 the death of the repressive King of Prussia promised the dawn of a new era in Berlin, and his successor persuaded Mendelssohn to take a post as the capital's music director. The composer left Leipzig with a heavy heart. In Berlin he met with bureaucratic difficulties and gradually withdrew from his obligations. His next achievement was to found the Leipzig Conservatory, which he built into Germany's foremost academy of music. In the meantime he continued his visits to England, which he always regarded as his second home, and became a firm favourite with Queen Victoria and Prince Albert who admired his urbanity as well as his compositions. In a typical burst of energy he composed his oratorio *Elijah* in a matter of months for the Birmingham Music Festival of 1846.

All this tireless activity was taking its toll. Public acclaim had never been more tumultuous, but Mendelssohn was driving himself too hard. In May 1847, as he was making his way home from his tenth visit to England, broken and exhausted, he was shattered to learn of the death of his beloved sister, Fanny. He never recovered from the blow. In October he had a slight stroke, and on 4 November he died. He was buried next to his sister. Amidst the public mourning, Cécile was alone. A few days after her husband's death she wrote:

There are corners of my mother-in-law's garden where I must martyr myself to be able to grasp what has happened. Here are the same trees, bower, branches, there is the ruined fountain, and they all still exist. Felix's grave bears a marble cross with his name. Behind it I have planted a lilac and a rosebush. I wanted to keep the mound free and green, it's always heaped with flowers and wreaths. I placed my tributes at his feet.

Six years later Cécile died, utterly inconsolable, at the age of 36.

In the last decade of his life, Mendelssohn focused his activities on the Leipzig Gewandhaus (below). Here, with typical energy and enthusiasm, he built up a distinguished orchestra, which became a model for all Europe. Under his leadership, they performed many major works that had previously been ignored – including Schubert's last symphony – and were graced with some of the finest soloists of the age. Through such selfless work, Mendelssohn created a lasting musical legacy, increasing the public's enjoyment of music.

COMPOSER'S LIFE

Mendelssohn's travels

Mendelssohn was an enthusiastic traveller. He was first sent abroad by his father on the 19th-century version of the Grand Tour to broaden his outlook before he took on permanent commitments. While being very well aware of the inconveniences and potential dangers of foreign travel, Mendelssohn seems to have enjoyed travel for its own sake – he liked new sights, sounds and experiences – but he also gained musical inspiration from seeing other lands. His visit to the Hebrides, in spite of terrible seasickness, inspired the Hebrides overture (better known as Fingal's Cave). Mendelssohn seems to have been loved and admired wherever he visited, and many people shared Queen Victoria's regret at his early death at the age of 38. The Queen's personal letter of condolence to the composer's young widow was a mark of this regret, and also signalled the popularity that Mendelssohn had achieved during his travels.

Guildhall, London/Bridgeman Art Library

COMPOSER'S LIFE
'If I rest, I rust'

With typical gusto Mendelssohn embarked upon an exhausting but fascinating series of tours, which, to judge from his impressions, contributed significantly to his spiritual and musical development.

The German motto of the title could well describe the enthusiasm, energy and fervour with which members of Mendelssohn's family went about their lives. Travel was always a very important factor for them. So it is no surprise that Mendelssohn himself was often on the move, giving concerts at home and abroad. However his first travels on his own as a young man were in 1829. His father sent him off on his solo travels so that he could broaden his outlook on life and establish himself as a man and an artist, before he took up permanent posts or made any other commitments in life. He advised Felix:

. . . closely to examine the various countries and to fix on one in which to live and work; to make his name and abilities known so that where he settled he should not be received as a stranger; and lastly to employ his good fortune in life, and the liberality of his father, in preparing the ground for future efforts.

By 1832, after a journey that had taken him through Scottish mist and London fog to the clear blue skies of Italy and back, he had accomplished all this and more. He had been so inspired by what he

had seen that he had translated his impressions into music – the 'Hebrides Overture', the 'Italian Symphony' and the 'Scottish Symphony' – though the last was not to be completed for another ten years. He had also settled on the country in which he wanted to live and work – his native Germany – despite the fact that, like Handel and Haydn before him, he had formed a special attachment to London. 'That smoky place is fated to be now and ever my favourite residence', he wrote to his sisters.

London life
London was where his Grand Tour in 1829 really began and he was to return to it nine times during his life. His love of travelling had already been awakened by trips to Paris and Switzerland as a boy with his energetic and enthusiastic family, but this was his first journey alone. His expectations of the British capital were high, as his friend Karl Klingemann, who was Secretary to the Hanoverian Legation in London, had already written enthusiastically about every aspect of his life there. Klingemann even relished the 'classical mutton, half-cooked vegetables and praise-worthy apple pie', despite the fact that he found

Mendelssohn disembarked in London (above) after a long and rough crossing from Hamburg. Progress was hampered by wind, fog and even a stop to repair the engine of the ship at the mouth of the Thames. Felix was sea-sick and cursed himself, the boat, England and his own recently-completed overture, **Calm Sea and Prosperous Voyage!**

Mendelssohn's high expectations of London were based on the enthusiastic impressions of his friend, Karl Klingemann (left), who was Secretary to the Hanoverian Legation in London.

Always an amusing and imaginative correspondent, Felix enjoyed sending hand-drawn notes (right).

English fare as heavy as the perpetual 'pea-souper' that enveloped the city. According to his reports, the ladies were pretty, the metropolis vast and music was flourishing. As for the English way of life:

The English comfort is the laziest fellow I ever met with. He gets up at ten o'clock, then he enters his cozy little room . . . a cheerful coal fire is blazing in the chimney, the water is boiling, the breakfast table laid, and everything upon it placed in proper symmetry – but with a special relish the eye rests upon an immeasurable newspaper, with leading articles, news, law suits, police reports and various scandal.

Since Mendelssohn's friend, the pianist Ignaz Moscheles, was also in London, enjoying great success in concert halls and salons, it was decided that Mendelssohn should join them both. He left Hamburg aboard the steamship *Attwood* on 18 April 1829. The sea was far from calm – the crossing took several days and Mendelssohn was violently ill.

This did not stop him from plunging straight into London life immediately he reached dry land. He went first to his lodgings in Portland Street then, in the company of Moscheles and Klingemann, on to the opera to see the first appearance of the celebrated opera singer Malibran, as Desdemona in Rossini's *Otello*.

I got a seat in the pit (half a guinea) – a large house, decorated with crimson, six tiers of boxes with crimson curtains, out of which peep the ladies, bedecked with great white feathers, chains, jewels of all kinds. An odour of pomade and perfume assails you as you enter, this gave me a headache: in the pit are all the gentlemen, with fresh-trimmed whiskers . . . Mme Malibran is a young woman, beautiful and splendidly made, her hair en troupet, full of fire and power, very coquettish . . .

This letter, the first of a long series to his family, runs on charged with excitement and breathlessly describes the welter of new impressions assailing his

keen senses from all sides.

Dressed in grey filigree stockings and olive coloured visiting gloves, Mendelssohn was introduced to society. Used to a less opulent Berlin, he was bowled over by the glitter of Georgian London. At a ball at Devonshire House, one of London's most fashionable venues, he spotted Wellington and Peel, marvelled at the Old Masters hanging on the walls and the candelabras wreathed in roses, the scent of thousands of flowers wafting through the room from the conservatory and the buffet spread with 'the fruits of all seasons'.

Balls, parties, dinners, the theatre, the opera followed one another in quick succession, but Mendelssohn was not always the perfectly mannered dandy. After dinner with the Prussian ambassador, he and two friends bought sausages to eat in the street and woke up the neighbourhood with an impromptu rendition of a three-part song.

Among the friends Mendelssohn made in London was Dr William Horsley, a composer of glees (unaccompanied songs for male singers). Horsley's daughters Fanny and Sophy glimpsed a very different side of the young composer to that which he presented when more on his guard.

Felix was very lachrymose and rushed four times in and out of the room in a very phrensied manner. I gazed at him for some time in such deep amaze that I am sure he at last perceived it. What an odd tempered creature he is. Mama and Mary think that Mendelssohn will never marry. I do, that is if he

In his first letter home, Felix told his family that he found London to be 'the most complicated monster on the face of the earth'. Regent Street (above) delighted him, with its bright arcades. He was fascinated by the shops, with their large signs, by the crowded stage coaches and by the passing show of people.

does not plague his mistress to death before the day arrives. He was dressed very badly and looked in want of the piece of soap and nailbrush that I have so often threatened to offer him.

The explanation for this 'phrensied' behaviour could be his frustration that Sir George Smart, one of the founders of the Philharmonic Society, had not fulfilled his promise (made in Berlin) of inviting Mendelssohn to perform. In anger and disappointment, the composer wrote home that Smart was an 'intriguing, deceitful and untruthful man'. However, the situation was resolved and the composer recovered his temper when, on 25 May, Smart invited him to the Argyll Rooms to conduct his C minor symphony.

It was a highly successful début and marked the beginning of the very warm relationship between Mendelssohn and the British public. The Philharmonic Society showed their appreciation by electing him an honorary member and he responded by dedicating the Symphony to them.

After a piano recital a few days later, Mendelssohn recorded with pleasure the bright summer hats of the ladies swaying in time to the music like a field of tulips, and exclaimed: 'By God, I play better here than in Berlin, and that's because people listen better.' More concerts followed, but the only commission that came his way was to write a hymn in celebration of the liberation of the natives of Ceylon, which he felt he was unable to accept. The prospect amused him, however, and he began signing

Apart from his musical activities in London, Mendelssohn was swept up in a whirl of social activity. His many letters of introduction gave him access to London society. Sought after by fashionable hostesses to attend parties and balls (above), he was overwhelmed by the splendour of the houses to which he was invited.

On his first evening in London, despite any lingering ill effects from his recent bout of sea-sickness, Felix rushed to the Italian Opera House in the Haymarket. The great attraction was the first performance of the celebrated opera singer, Madame Malibran (right), as Desdemona in Rossini's Otello.

his letters 'Composer to the Island of Ceylon'.

His greatest success came on 13 July with the charity concert for Silesia, which he arranged in collaboration with the House of Lords. The concert was sold out and hundreds of people had to be turned away, such was the draw of the combined names of Moscheles, Malibran and Henriette Sontag, all of whom had been prevailed upon to perform under the young genius's baton.

Scottish interlude

This triumph behind him, Mendelssohn set off in late July with Klingemann for a trip to Scotland. It was the heyday of coach travel – the horses were changed about every ten miles so that they could keep up a steady pace. The travellers proceeded in relative comfort (earlier coaches had no windows and doors, only a curtain to keep off the weather), and stopped three times a day for refreshments. Coaches travelled through the night – in 1829, 5000 coaches worked 12,000 miles of road every 24 hours and it took 30,000 men and 150,000 horses to operate the system. Because the service was so labour-intensive, fares were quite high – the journey as far as Stamford took ten hours and cost £3. 10s – but those with a more robust constitution could travel as 'outsiders' on top of the coach for about half price. Outsiders often had more than the elements to contend with. The expression 'dropping off' dates from the days when travellers were liable to be lulled to sleep by the motion of the coach and literally dropped off it!

Mendelssohn and Klingemann stopped off in York and Durham before arriving in Edinburgh on Sunday 28 July. Felix recalled the scene:

many Highlanders came in costume from church, victoriously leading their sweethearts in their Sunday best and casting magnificent and important

looks over the world; with long red beards, tartan plaids, bonnets and feathers, naked knees and their bagpipes in their hands . . .

The two intrepid travellers climbed 'Arthur's Seat', steep rocks that gave them a splendid view of the Edinburgh skyline which Mendelssohn, true to form, recorded in his sketch pad. Though they spent only three days in Edinburgh, one of which was taken up by a visit to Sir Walter Scott, it was a highly profitable stay, providing much inspiration for the composer. After a twilight visit to the ruined chapel of Mary Stuart at Holyrood House he recorded that he had found the beginning of his 'Scotch' Symphony.

The visit to Sir Walter Scott was memorable only in Klingemann's invented report of it. In a letter beginning 'Most astonished friends! O most amazed readers!' he describes the great man's transports of

Coach travel (above) was in its heyday at the time Mendelssohn set out on his travels. Travellers were fairly comfortable inside the coach although early coaches had no windows and doors and only a curtain kept the weather at bay.

In Edinburgh, Felix and Klingemann climbed 'Arthur's Seat'. Felix described the view of Edinburgh (above left, from the observatory): '... the castle, like a bird's nest on a cliff; beyond the castle come meadows, then hills... then a mountain rather more stern on which towers Stirling Castle; then blue distance begins ...'. From Edinburgh they went north to the Highlands (above) where '... smoky huts were stuck on cliffs, ugly women looked through window-holes, cattle herds with Rob Roys now and then blocked up the way, mighty mountains were sticking up to their knees in the clouds, and looked out again from the top'.

After travelling through the Highlands and a visit to the Hebrides, Klingemann and Mendelssohn went to Glasgow. Here they parted company; Felix continued to Wales (right) to visit the Taylor family, at Coed du, near Holywell.

delight at meeting him. The reality was somewhat different, as Mendelssohn confessed:

We found Sir Walter in the act of leaving Abbotsford, stared at him like fools, drove 80 miles and lost a day for the sake of at best one half hour of superficial conversation ... we were out of humour with great men, with ourselves, with the world, with everything. It was a bad day.

But the next day they were able to laugh at their escapade and started out on their Highland journey in high spirits. They travelled partly by coach and cart and partly on foot and spent much time admiring the rugged mountains, steep waterfalls and heather-covered heaths.

At night they took refuge from the wind and the rain by the fireside of an inn, where they donned 'Scotch wooden shoes', ate honey and potato cakes and drank whisky. And while Mendelssohn sketched and Klingemann wrote verses, they listened to the servants singing drunken songs in Gaelic and laughing. Yet 'in spite of the servants' noise and the door-banging, there is repose. It is quiet and lonely here! I might say that the stillness rings through the noise.'

On 7 August they had their first view of the Hebrides, and although the general form and colour of the 'Hebrides' overture was suggested by the sight of Fingal's Cave (the name by which Mendelssohn's Opus 26 is also known), it was while looking across from Oban at the islands that the first bars of the piece came to him.

The boat trip to Fingal's Cave on the remote island of Staffa was a rough one, and Mendelssohn was again dreadfully sea-sick – a condition not alleviated by the presence of a yellow mulatto cook frying stale ham on deck.

After a visit to Iona they returned south via Inverary to the sun and civilization of Glasgow,

where they observed the Industrial Revolution in full swing during a visit to a cotton mill. Town life was a welcome contrast after what Klingemann called 'the wretchedness and the comfortless inhospitality of the country'.

The travellers now parted company and Mendelssohn continued to Wales and the home of the Taylor family, at Coed du, where he had an introduction. The daughters, Susan, Honoria and Anne, were soon captivated by his quick mind and modest charm. They were not familiar with his music, but quickly grew to love it, marvelling at the way new pieces suggested themselves to him.

Mendelssohn was prevented from returning to Berlin for his sister Fanny's wedding by an accident to his knee. His convalescence was spent mainly in London, with a few weeks at the Norwood home of Sir Thomas Attwood, the distinguished organist and church composer. He eventually returned to Berlin in December where he arrived in good time for his parents' silver wedding anniversary.

The following May he resumed his travels, this

time setting off for Italy. On the way he visited Goethe in Weimar, then passed through Salzburg, Vienna and Budapest, where he witnessed the coronation of King Ferdinand V of Hungary.

Italian holiday

On 10 October 1830 he reached Venice. 'Italy at last! and what I have all my life considered as the greatest possible felicity, is now begun, and I am basking in it.' His early letters from Italy are full of wonder and infectious happiness.

In Venice he was impressed above all else by the painting of Titian, and in particular, his *Assumption,* but he was equally susceptible to the Bridge of Sighs, St. Mark's Square and the special flavour of local festivals, of which he was always a sensitive observer. From Venice he journeyed to Florence and then on to Rome for the winter. His first sight of Rome was 'in bright and shining moonlight'. He rented a sunny apartment equipped with a good Viennese grand

Overjoyed to be in Italy at last, Mendelssohn's watercolour (right) sums up his romantic northern view of the light of a southern climate. He saw Florence 'at a distance in the valley, the blue city'.

Archiv für Kunst und Geschichte

Petit Palais/Bulloz

Joachim Blauel/Artothek

Mendelssohn was amazed by the beauty he found all around him in Italy, but was disturbed by the poverty and misery he saw as well – like that of this beggar woman (above). 'I'm pained',
he wrote, 'by the incredible mass of beggars who haunt one at every step and surround one's carriage as soon as it stops . . .'.

From Florence he went to Rome where he settled for the winter of 1830–31. Here he worked on compositions until noon, then took himself off to see monuments like the Forum (left) in the afternoons. 'Rome's past seems to me like history itself. Its monuments inspire, whether they make one feel serious or gay. It is satisfying to think that human beings can accomplish something that continues to refresh and strengthen them after thousands of years,' he wrote.

piano and quickly established a daily routine. Every day he composed until noon, working on Goethe's *Walpurgisnacht* and his 'Italian' Symphony, which he described as 'sportive'. After lunch, with characteristic thoroughness, he systematically visited all the sights of the city.

The evenings were spent socializing, mainly with expatriate Germans whom he met through his father's banking business and entertained with his piano playing. He also got to know the artist Horace Vernet, the sculptor Thorwaldsen and, when he returned from Naples, Berlioz, whose music he eventually came to respect, but whose emotional excesses made him wary.

When, that winter, the Pope died, Mendelssohn was appalled by the irreverence of the people:

It is quite revolting to see their unconcern about the death of the Pope, and their unseemly merriment during the ceremonies. I myself saw the corpse lying in state, and the priests standing round incessantly whispering and laughing; and at this moment when masses are being said for his soul, they are in the very same church hammering away at the scaffolding of the catafalque...

It was no wonder such an apathetic people had no

Kunsthalle, Hamburg/Robert Harding Picture Library

The Caffè Greco in the Via Condotti, Rome (above) was a tavern frequented by many German painters, of whom Mendelssohn had a very low opinion. Known as the 'Nazarenes' they were inspired by religious ideals and the works of the young Raphael. Mendelssohn did mix with some of the more distinguished members of the group, but his view of the hangers-on echoed that of Byron, who commented that if they would 'cut their hair, convert it into brushes, and paint like Raphael' rather than merely looking like him, it would be more to the point.

In spring 1831 Felix set off again – this time to Naples (left) and the islands of Ischia and Capri.

Archiv für Kunst und Geschichte

regard for music and actually took out pencils and knives to inscribe their insignificant names on priceless works of art. He was disturbed by the Italians' profound ignorance of classical music and the bad standards of musicianship he found all over Italy. Orchestras played out of tune; to hear a group of people singing was no more melodious than hearing a violent quarrel, and not a note of Beethoven or Mozart was played; his own fervent admiration of the classics was greeted with scorn or amusement.

Florence, he had discovered, was full of scoundrels and he had to use all his poise and confidence and stretch his Italian to the limits to avoid being robbed

at every turn. Everywhere he met 'disgusting crooks ... finally I became dizzy with all the cheating. I no longer knew to whom they were lying, so whatever they said I'd protest and declare "I'm not going to pay".'

When spring came, he hurried to Naples and the islands of Ischia and Capri. The beauty of the bay and the surrounding countryside did not disappoint him, and he found the inspiration he needed to complete the 'Italian' Symphony. But his energy was sapped by the incessant wind, the *sirocco,* and he was depressed by the hordes of beggars who followed him everywhere, complaining that they were dying of hunger. The oppressive climate, he concluded, could

Mendelssohn made his way back to Germany via Switzerland and the Swiss countryside (above), delighted him. He could not understand why the poet Goethe, whom he had met in Weimar 10 years before, had only been inspired by all this wonder to 'a few feeble poems and still feebler letters'.

When he was a young man, Goethe (right), shown at the window of his lodgings in Rome, had travelled to many of the places later visited by Felix. Felix read Goethe's Italian journal and poems, and found his own thoughts reflected in them.

support only grandees and beggars – both types of person having nothing much to do but lie about.

After this it was time to head northwards again. He stopped off in Rome for Holy Week, and Milan. Here he made the acquaintance of Dorothea von Ertmann, who entertained him with anecdotes of her old admirer Beethoven, and Karl Mozart, whom *he* entertained by playing some of his father's music.

Switzerland, with its 'thrifty cleanliness', was a relief after the dirt and fleas of Italy. 'I think this kind of domestic comfort is only to be found among those who speak the German tongue,' boasted the composer. It did not matter to him that he was on foot in torrential rain, that bridges had been swept away and he had to ford roaring streams until his shoes shrank. He was so overwhelmed by the natural beauty of the places he visited that he found it hard to believe it had inspired Goethe to only a few poems and letters.

In September he arrived in Munich, where he was received at court, and the following winter saw him in Paris. He plunged into its dazzling social life, meeting Chopin, Liszt, Paganini and Meyerbeer, but found the constant talk of politics tedious – the Revolution of the previous summer was still very much in people's minds. His *Reformation* Symphony was rejected by the Conservatoire, and this did nothing to further his appreciation of Parisian music, which was dominated by Meyerbeer. 'I do cordially hate the present licentious style', he wrote, and 'I take music in a very serious light.'

Another brief visit to London intervened before he finally settled in Germany taking up his first appointment as conductor to the Leipzig Gewandhaus in 1835. For the next ten years this was to be the main focus of his activities.

Although his Grand Tour formally ended in the spring of 1832, he was nevertheless a constant visitor to England. The climax of these visits was his meeting with Queen Victoria and Prince Albert

Carnavalet, Paris/Lauros-Giraudon

Mendelssohn cared little for Paris on his first visit there with his father in 1825. However, he found it a more congenial city on his return in the winter of 1831. He went frequently to the theatre (left), greatly admiring Léontine Fay the actress.

In Paris he plunged into a dazzling social and musical life, attending glittering soirées (below), going to the Opéra, where Meyerbeer, whose work he deplored, was all the rage, and yet finding the time to relax with friends.

Carnavalet, Paris/Lauros-Giraudon

in 1842. Mendelssohn was in England conducting amongst other things his 'Scottish' symphony, recently completed. He had an introduction to Prince Albert from the King of Prussia.

During his second meeting with the Prince the 23 year-old Queen came into the room wearing a housedress. Seeing that the wind had blown manuscript all over the floor, she bent to retrieve them, and Albert and Mendelssohn helped. Then the two men took it in turns to play. Later they moved to the Queen's sitting room to find one of Mendelssohn's songs for her to sing.

After she had sung, first a song that Mendelssohn admitted Fanny, his sister, had written, then one of his own, Victoria recorded in her journal that they gave the composer two themes on which to extemporize:

'Rule Britannia' and the Austrian National Anthem . . . really I have never heard anything so beautiful; the way in which he blended them both together and changed over from one to the other was quite wonderful as well as the exquisite harmony and feelings he puts into the variations, and the powerful rich chords and modulations, which reminded one of all his beautiful compositions.

When Mendelssohn died in November 1847, Victoria wrote in her diary:

We were horrified, astounded and distressed to read in the papers of the death of Mendelssohn, the greatest musical genius since Mozart & the most amiable man.

She followed this by a letter of condolence to the composer's widow, an unprecedented gesture that showed how much Mendelssohn had done to advance the social status of the musician in Europe.

The portrait and part of the obituary (right) of Mendelssohn which appeared in The Illustrated London News *on 13 November 1847, marking his death on 4 November 1847. The pace at which he lived his life and the enthusiasm and energy which he devoted to his music, family and friends finally took their toll of him. When returning in May 1847 from his tenth visit to England, he heard of the death of his beloved sister, Fanny. This, coupled with exhaustion, led to a stroke in October from which he never recovered.*

triumphant reception in London last spring now brings a melancholy feeling in its recollection.

On the 5th of last October, Mendelssohn was struck with apoplexy ; and, although, as younger patients usually do, he struggled against the malady, it gradually overcame him, by frequent repetition, and he expired on the 4th instant, in his 39th year, thus bringing to an un-

THE LATE DR. FELIX MENDELSSOHN BARTHOLDY.

timely termination a life graced by every private virtue, and illustrated by talents that class him among the greatest of his era.

The Illustrated London News

Listener's guide

Any analysis of the life and times of a great composer cannot ignore his music, and this section examines in detail some of Mendelssohn's greatest and best-known works: the Violin Concerto, the Italian Symphony, and his overtures, including Fingal's Cave and A Midsummer Night's Dream. Together with sections on specific aspects of musical development of relevance to the composer (for example, Mendelssohn's rôle in the 19th-century revival of Johann Sebastian Bach's music), the descriptions of the pieces of music can be read independently as part of an assessment of Mendelssohn's musical achievements. However, for the fullest appreciation of this great composer's music, the programme notes are better read before going to a live performance or while listening to the recorded music. Suggestions for further listening are given within the text, and the Bibliography and the short descriptions of the lives and works of contemporary composers on page 110 suggest other areas of study.

Great interpreters

Ruggiero Ricci (violinist)

Born in San Francisco in 1918, Ricci studied with André Persinger from the age of eight, making his débuts in San Francisco and New York in 1928 and 1929 respectively, as a child prodigy, playing the Mendelssohn Violin Concerto.

His studies continued during the early 30s with Michel Piastro and Georg Kulenkampff before he embarked on his first triumphant European tour in 1932. Still only 15, he returned to his studies with Persinger, with additional tuition from Paul Stassevich, blossoming by his early 20s into a highly accomplished virtuoso violinist.

Just prior to and after World War II he established his repertoire and quickly became accepted in the public eye as an unparalleled performer of the bravura-style piece for violin. In the last couple of decades he has recorded regularly as well as touring the classical centres of the world. As a result, he has come to be accepted as one of the handful of truly great violinists to have emerged in this century.

Ricci is the possessor of a rich and deeply expressive tone, and this technique is always at the service of the music. All manner of complexities of execution ceased to be a problem for him many years ago and he is a true master. His performances of the 19th-century virtuoso Paganini's violin works, which are of the utmost technical difficulty, are especially treasured by his followers.

Since the early 70s he has spent an increasing amount of his time teaching young musicians in specialist classes, latterly at the famous Juilliard School in New York.

Claudio Abbado (conductor)

Abbado is one of the few conductors from the generation since World War II to have successfully established himself as a

The conductor, Claudio Abbado (above). The violinist, Ruggiero Ricci (left).

major force. As such, he is carrying forward the great tradition of the older men who had dominated the world's stages for most of this century.

He was born in 1933 in Milan, and decided at the age of eight that he wanted to be a conductor. Having trained at the Verdi Conservatory in Milan in both piano and composition, he moved on in 1955 to the Vienna Academy of Music.

True to his childhood decision, he concentrated on a conducting career and in 1958 conducted at provincial concerts in Italy. After a relatively slow start, he won the Dmitri Mitropoulos Prize in 1963, which carried as a reward a short attachment to the New York Philharmonic. This, plus his exposure at the 1965 Salzburg festival, added to his growing reputation. His début at La Scala, Milan, occurred in the same year, and by 1968 he had been appointed permanent conductor there. Later, he was made artistic director. During his time with the company he developed it into a superb musical and dramatic unit and considerably enlarged its repertoire.

His long relationship with the London Symphony Orchestra, starting with his appointment as principal guest conductor in 1972, matured into a clearly special understanding which in turn led to his position being confirmed as principal conductor in 1979. Abbado has interpreted composers as disparate as Bizet, Mendelssohn, Verdi, Berg and Ligeti. In recent years he has shown a particular affinity with Mahler.

FURTHER LISTENING

Mendelssohn orchestral works

Symphony no. 5 in D ('Reformation')
In this his final Symphony, Mendelssohn portrayed through music the titanic struggle of ideals and spirit between the Catholic Church and the reforming Martin Luther. Apart from a charming and graceful second movement, the music is wholly taken up with expressing the conflicts between these opposing forces in brilliantly-scored and developed musical motifs.

Symphony no. 3 in A Minor ('Scottish')
In 1829, Mendelssohn toured Scotland and was immensely impressed by what he saw This Symphony is only one of the works which grew out of his enchantment with this land, but it is perhaps the most impressive. A brilliantly worked and integrated piece of musical structure, it possesses an abundance of melodies and themes of beauty and substance. The lilting opening theme of the final movement reveals especially a Scottish influence and this impression is enhanced as the movement, and the Symphony, come to a rousing close.

Piano Concerto no. 1 in G Minor
Although he was only 22 when he wrote his First Piano Concerto, Mendelssohn was no stranger to the form and composed a smoothly-flowing and utterly assured three-movement work. It is full of attractive musical dialogue between the piano and orchestra. While there is plenty of virtuosity for the piano soloist, the work still shows itself to be a model of poise and symmetry.

Violin Concerto and 'Italian' Symphony

These are two of Mendelssohn's most enchanting and endearing works. The Violin Concerto is fresh and spontaneous in mood, while the Fourth Symphony is a vivid memento of Italy.

Underlying the overall carefree nature of the Violin Concerto are passages of intense reflection (right). The soloist hovers between moods of utter exuberance and wistful yearning.

The composition of the Violin Concerto did not come easily to the young Mendelssohn (right). He was at pains to create a work that would satisfy the most stringent technical demands as well as his own musical vision. The result represents one of the summits of his achievement. The great violinist Joachim, who played the work frequently, placed it in the context of the other great German violin concertos: Beethoven's made the 'fewest concessions'; Brahms's came close to Beethoven's in its 'seriousness'; but 'the dearest of them all, the heart's jewel' was Mendelssohn's.

Violin Concerto in E minor, op. 64

In July 1838, Mendelssohn wrote to his friend the violinist Ferdinand David:

I should like to write a violin concerto for you this winter. The beginning of one in E minor runs constantly through my thoughts, giving me no peace.

In their subsequent correspondence, David encouraged the composer to proceed with the work and expressed the desire that it should be of the utmost brilliance. Doubtless by this he meant that it should be 'showy' — but this type of music was foreign to Mendelssohn's make-up and he became torn between his natural musicality and the desire to satisfy his

friend's demands. Consequently, the Concerto took several years to complete, years during which the composer sought David's advice continually on matters of detail. Changes were even made after David had given the first performance on 13 March 1845.

Programme notes

It is difficult to believe that a work of such spontaneous freshness underwent so agonizing a gestation, but evidence of the extraordinary care Mendelssohn put into its composition will be found, not only in

the beautifully proportioned melodies, but also in its novel formal layout. Unlike its traditional models, which begin with an extended orchestral passage, this Concerto has a mere bar and a half of introduction before the entrance of the soloist. Furthermore, the cadenza, traditionally left to the soloist to compose himself is written out in full by Mendelssohn and brought forward to a position between the development and the recapitulation.

First movement – Allegro molto appassionato
The soloist's opening theme is passionate, yearning and intense. It is played wholly on the E string and spends nearly all its time well above the stave:

Example 1

The orchestra, meanwhile, plays a completely subordinate role, accompanying the theme and providing punctuation at the end. Immediately, the soloist launches in to a second idea mainly in *triplets* (three notes played in the time usually occupied by two) at the end of which the opening theme is handed over to the orchestra. Soon two new ideas are introduced, the second of which is taken up by the soloist who extends it considerably in intricate *passage-work* — a short section of the musical composition for the soloist's display.

At last the music calms and the real second subject appears on flutes and clarinets, marked *tranquillo* and *pp* (tranquilly and very quietly) over a low G on the violin, its lowest note. This lovely melody holds the attention for some time until the soloist reintroduces the first theme, its two components being combined and repeated obsessively.

At the height of the ensuing passionate outburst, amid fierce and prolonged chords from the orchestra, the music moves into the development section, the soloist dramatically intoning the first notes of the opening theme which are now given a forward-springing, rhythmic impulse. As the development continues, this first theme's possibilities are put exhaustively to the test, its elements separated one from the

Bildarchiv Preussischer Kulturbesitz

Whistler 'The Little White Girl: Symphony in White no. 2' The Tate Gallery, London

other and reassembled in new ways; both the soloist and the orchestra seem to delight in the game of making transformations as the mood changes from agitation to tranquillity.

There is a sudden *crescendo* at the height of which the soloist spins off into the carefully written-out cadenza. This is of a brilliance that surely pleased even David, the ace virtuoso, for it demands the utmost skill in its rapid ascents to top B, then top C, and finally top E; nerve in tackling the perilous upward leaps; and superlative bow control in the quicksilver arpeggios. It is while the soloist is engaged in a whirling series of arpeggios that the orchestra steals in with the soft restatement of the opening melody – a truly thrilling moment.

Much of the recapitulation that now follows is reshaped, revealing at every turn new and unexpected facets of the melodies. The second main subject, previously in G major, now sounds out in a radiant E major, the soloist's low held note amended accordingly from G to E as the woodwind colours are gloriously enhanced by the new key. But clouds drift across the scene as the music earnestly heads for the prolonged orchestral chords which now announce the coda. With a gradual increase in tempo to *presto* (quick), the soloist dashes off rapid passage-work and *double-stops* (the playing of two strings simultaneously), landing at length on top E. Then, a series of chords brings the first movement to a decisive end.

Second movement – Andante

From these chords at the end of the first movement, one bassoon note is drawn out: a B rises to C and a brief introduction brings the entry of the soloist in one of Mendelssohn's most timeless and ravishing melodies. For many bars this sublime tune unfolds while the orchestra, confined to strings and the most mellow of the woodwinds (clarinets and bassoons), supports discreetly.

In the centre of the movement occurs an extraordinary passage, full of anguish and foreboding. Horns, trumpets, drums and the rest of the woodwind join the orchestra to announce this section with a tune combining strength with resignation. Then the violin enters, intoning this tune in constant double-stopping. An anguished climax occurs, but the tragedy is not dissipated. The agitated rippling motion which has been maintained throughout this central section now continues, as if carrying the reminder that beauty cannot exist without the presence of stress. The end of the movement returns to the perfect tranquillity of the opening as the solo violin soars aloft and gently descends again.

Third movement – Allegretto non troppo – Allegro molto vivace

After a short introduction, the Finale is announced by a fanfare on bassoons, brass and drums. This is answered by a bantering upward flourish by the soloist, the sequence being immediately repeated. This flourish marks the beginning of the violinist's first solo. The pace is fast and a frequent direction in the score is *leggiero* (light, swift, delicate). Woodwind follow and dance around the soloist's lead as the music runs breathlessly and joyously, the upward flourish being tossed from violin to clarinets and back again in sheer jubilation.

At the top of a precipitate rush up the scale, the soloist encounters a new theme on full orchestra:

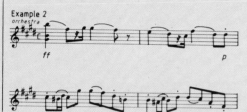

acclaims it with a squeal of delight and then runs away with it. It is soon taken back by the orchestra, however, as it appears quietly and unexpectedly here and there while the soloist scampers about as if searching for it. Unsuccessful, the soloist alternates swift arpeggios with pizzicato chords (perhaps the nearest the music approaches to a shrug), apparently unconcerned now as to the fate of the second theme; a perfectly good first theme awaits and it is time to return to it.

After a brief statement, the violin announces a new idea in long notes: a gravely beautiful melody that, for all its poise, is unable to withstand the banter from the rest of the orchestra and capitulates to the first theme. But the instant it does so the orchestral strings adopt this melody, leaving the soloist to play with the first theme. The two elements are now properly combined as the recapitulation enters.

In due time the second theme (Example 2) returns, leading the music inescapably towards what should be the ultimate showpiece of all concertos: the final cadenza. The ground is prepared by a series of ascending trills from the soloist, but a clarinet playfully repeats the violinist's first flourish, flutes suggest the first theme, and the soloist, weary of holding trills, scampers down the scale relieved to be absolved from the responsibility of providing a showy cadenza in such a boisterous context. A final scurry brings the Concerto to a vivacious close.

Ferdinand David, the violinist-friend for whom Mendelssohn wrote the Violin Concerto, wanted a work that would allow him to show off his brilliant virtuosity. And Mendelssohn gave him plenty of scope for bravura display: thrilling upward leaps, whirling arpeggios and heart-stopping ascents all demand the utmost skill and artistic flair (right).

Understanding music: the Bach revival

Fame eluded Bach during his lifetime, and though he yearned for it, he was remarkably reluctant to publish his work. He took instead to distributing his music to friends, colleagues, other musicians and patrons.

After his death in 1750, his successors rejected the artistic principles Bach had stood for and attacked his work as technically skilful but turgid and lacking in expression. His music was rarely performed in public.

Fortunately, it was a different matter in private. Among those who collected Bach's own manuscripts were Johann Philipp Kirnberger, violinist and composer, and Princess Amalia, sister of Frederick the Great, at whose court in Potsdam Bach's second son, Carl Philipp Emanuel, was a virtuoso harpsichordist. In 1762 another son, Johann Christian, went to London where the musicologist Charles Burney (father of the writer Fanny Burney) heard him perform several times. By 1772 Burney had acquired a copy of Bach's *The Well-Tempered Clavier Book 1,* and the composer and pianist Muzio Clementi had a copy of *Book 2* which he rehearsed ceaselessly.

Between 1784 and 1787, C. P. E. Bach published a collected edition of his father's chorales, though not the cantatas which featured them. In 1802, Clementi took his Irish protégé, John Field, on a musical tour of Europe where they dazzled audiences with Bach's music. A London friend of Field's, George Pinto, introduced Bach's preludes and fugues to the organist Samuel Wesley; overwhelmed by what he described as

Mendelssohn performed many Bach works at the Leipzig Gewandhaus where he was Director.

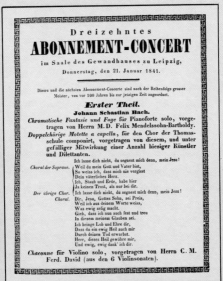

Bach's 'superhuman genius', Wesley became an immediate evangelist for Bach — by 1808, he had organized a season of Bach concerts at Surrey Chapel. Therefore, though Bach's music was by no means forgotten, it could not yet be called popular.

The increasing interest in the past which was a feature of the Romantic age, along with the need to instil pride in German national traditions after the exploits of Napoleon, and a religious revival, all contributed to a growing general appreciation of Bach. In Vienna during the 1780s, Baron von Swieten, a friend of several musicians in Frederick the Great's court, held musical evenings at his home featuring baroque music, many of which included works by Bach. Forkel, one of von Swieten's friends, in 1802 published a full biography of Bach in the most eulogistic and patriotic terms. The revival was now steadily gathering momentum.

However, it was really through the efforts of Mendelssohn that popularity was eventually achieved. In Berlin, Carl Zelter, who had founded the Berlin Singakademie in 1791, was actively promoting the revival of some of Bach's choral church music, but it was not until 1829 that he was persuaded to put on a public performance of Bach's *St Matthew Passion.* As conductor he chose his own pupil, Mendelssohn. The performance was a great success, and four years later, the Singakademie performed the *St John Passion.*

Meanwhile, Mendelssohn visited London in 1829 and 1832 and played Bach's music, notably on the organ at St Paul's Cathedral, to great acclaim. His former teacher, Ignaz Moscheles, continued to play Bach at London concerts for years afterwards, and Mendelssohn's friendship with Queen Victoria and Prince Albert influenced them to insist on performances of Bach at Buckingham Palace and Windsor Castle. Finally, in 1849, William Sterndale Bennett, Mendelssohn's pupil and a friend of Schumann, founded the Bach Society at which, five years later, the first performance in England of the *St Matthew Passion* took place.

Schumann continued to press for the publication of all Bach's works, and by 1850, a century after Bach's death, the German equivalent of the Bach Society had begun to compile it, a task which took 50 years to complete. And it was not till 1950 that the more precise catalogue of Bach's works, the *Bach-Werke-Verzeichnis* was published to give us the now familiar BWV numbers to his works.

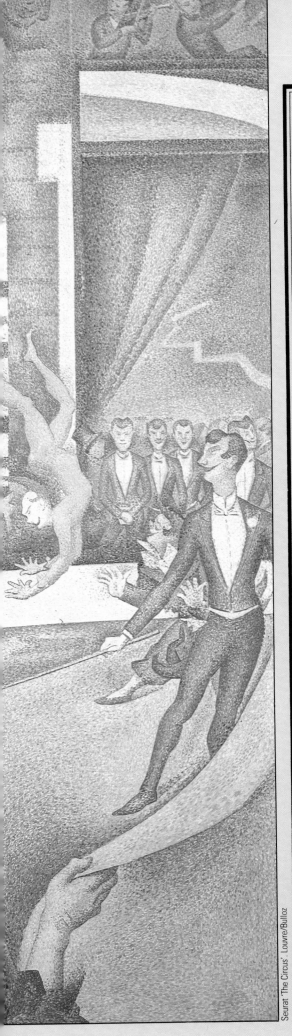

Seurat: 'The Circus'. Louvre/Bulloz

Bildarchiv Preussischer Kulturbesitz

Symphony no. 4 in A major, op. 90 ('Italian')

In November 1832, the Philharmonic Society of London offered Mendelssohn one hundred guineas for 'a Symphony, an Overture, and a Vocal Piece'. What today seems a meagre sum of money for three major works of art was, at that time, an average-to-good payment. For Mendelssohn, however, the eminently successful son of a wealthy family, it made little impact upon his fortune. Nevertheless, he tackled the job with alacrity, and the 'Italian' Symphony was brought to completion. It received its first performance in London on 13 May 1833.

The 'Italian' Symphony is universally known as 'no. 4', yet this number, as with so many others in music literature, is totally misleading. Between 1821 and 1823, when he was 12 to 14 years old, Mendelssohn had composed a dozen complete symphonies, most of which were published for the first time as recently as 1971. The Symphony now known as 'no. 1' appeared in 1824, but Mendelssohn himself referred to it as 'no. 13'. The correct chronological order of the last four symphonies is as follows: no. 5 (the 'Reformation', 1832), no. 4 (the 'Italian', 1833), no. 2 (the 'Hymn of Praise', 1840), and no. 3 (the 'Scottish', 1842).

Programme notes

After his visit to Scotland, which resulted eventually in the 'Scottish' Symphony and the famous 'Hebrides' Overture ('Fingal's Cave'), Mendelssohn toured the main centres of Italy from October 1830 to August 1831: Venice, Florence, Rome (where the 'Italian' Symphony was begun), Naples, Pompeii, Genoa and Milan. His keen ear and sensitive feeling for atmosphere enabled him to store material for his new symphony, but its actual composition did not come easily to him. He complained at one point that its creation was costing him his 'most bitter moments'.

Even after its completion, Mendelssohn planned to make revisions, particularly to the finale. Perhaps he intended to add an A major section at the end of that movement (which is in A minor), so that the key pattern might be closed neatly. We may consider it a lucky stroke that other commitments prevented him from doing

so: as it stands, the Symphony is so satisfying and well rounded, that it is difficult to believe that alterations would have done anything other than impair the balance of the work. It is a faultless expression of joy and a vivid memento of his months in Italy.

First movement – Allegro vivace

With a sharp chord, like the crack of a starter's pistol, the first movement is off at a sprint, chattering woodwind and horns setting a hot pace against which the violins sweep the main theme along. A moment – no more – of hesitation, then flutes, oboes and horns enter with the fanfare-like reminder of the first theme. But the wind instruments are unable to progress beyond that opening phrase and, after they have repeated it several times, it is snatched back by the violin like a baton in a relay race and played again, its ending changed.

In an exciting sequence, strings alternate with the rest of the orchestra in a brief shuttling phrase; one can picture two voluble Italian women arguing over some bargain in a Roman market place. Further reminders of the main melody at length bring a series of smoothly ascending phrases (woodwind, then strings) that lead into the second melody:

Example 3

This graceful idea is extended over many bars, slowly smoothing the ebullient music into a moment of repose – a much-needed breathing space after the eventful opening paragraph. All at once, though, a solo clarinet signals a reminder of the first theme and the orchestra surges forward with renewed vigour. The exposition ends with a return to the first theme, and is then repeated from the moment at which it was first heard, at the start of the Symphony.

The end of the exposition, called the *codetta* (little tail), is foreshortened on its second appearance, the music moving breathlessly into the development section with the rising woodwind phrases heard against pattering string triplets. Almost immediately, Mendelssohn introduces a new melody: a dance-like, capricious idea that never develops beyond its four-bar limits:

The first movement of the 'Italian' Symphony (autograph score – above) has a wonderful freshness and spontaneity. A lively dialogue between the strings and the rest of the orchestra conjures up a picture of a bustling Italian market place (left).

In contrast, the slow second movement is based on a religious procession (right) that Mendelssohn saw in Naples. It opens with a wailing motif, suggestive of a funeral cortège. Mendelssohn charts its progress, while watching the mourners gradually recede.

Example 4
2nd violins

Instead, once its arrival has been acclaimed by woodwind, trumpets and drums, it is fragmented and turned into a quiet, almost furtive, *fugato* by the strings – that is, in the style of a *fugue,* where melodies overlap in imitation of each other.

The rest of the orchestra becomes restless at this interloper's irrelevant display. Amid mounting tension the first theme is restated by all the woodwind, answered by all the brass supported by drums, and the violins are forced to acquiesce. Defiantly, the dance-like melody (Example 4) fights back, *fortissimo,* and considerable stress enters the music as this third theme becomes entangled with the first.

Baffled, the music subsides, apparently considering how best to reintroduce the first theme and bring in the recapitulation that formal musical grammar demands, but without intervention from that unwanted gate-crasher (Example 4). A solo oboe, *pianissimo* (very soft), comes to the rescue. Like a cooling hand on a fevered brow, it gently restates the start of the opening theme in long notes, and the music, reassured, launches into the recapitulation. This proceeds with minor changes, one of them being that the second theme (Example 3), is now played on violas and cellos. By a magical stroke of

The graceful and restrained third movement was partially inspired by Goethe's humorous poem Lili's Park *(illustrated above), written for the lovely Lili Schönemann. It is a stately minuet (right), very subtly scored, of the type that Haydn included in his symphonies.*

scoring in which Mendelssohn places his cellos *above* the violas, a satisfyingly rich sound is achieved.

The melody rises through the orchestra and, as before, brings response, but whereas in the exposition the clarinet had interrupted the repose, now it is that capricious melody (Example 4) which impishly returns, holding the stage obstinately. Only the forceful restatement of the first subject subdues it, but it has now become an integral part of the first theme and, having joined the race in the middle, is present at the end to participate unsportingly in the victory. Before the close, however, yet another idea is introduced with great subtlety. It is a rising figure on flute over a pizzicato bassline: a clear foretaste of the second movement.

Second movement – Andante con moto

When in Naples, Mendelssohn is reported to have witnessed a religious procession;

the slow movement, in the devout key of D minor, is a stylized suggestion of this experience. It opens with a kind of wailing sound, as if of mourners. Perhaps it was a funeral cortège the composer saw. The procession then begins, the theme imaginatively scored for oboe, two bassoons and violas over a marching bassline. Another statement, on violins, is accompanied by a delicate descant for two flutes. Then comes the second half of the melody which had already been hinted at near the end of the first movement; this, too, is then ornamented by flutes.

The next idea (on violins) is derived from the opening wail and leads to a consoling passage of great beauty. The wail returns, and the material is restated without complications until, at the very end, as the mourners seem to pass out of sight, the sound of the procession is lost in the distance.

Third movement – Con moto moderato

Beethoven took the Haydn symphonic minuet and turned it into a scherzo, transferring a courtly or rustic dance into a headlong movement that not even the rashest dancer would attempt to step to. Once, however, in his Symphony no. 8, Beethoven reintroduced the stately minuet, and it would seem that Mendelssohn turned to this as a model for his 'Italian' Symphony. This is not inappropriate, for Italy had been the home of a particularly graceful species of minuet early in the 18th century. Could Mendelssohn have heard some of these ancient dances during his visit? Mendelssohn's other source of

inspiration seems to have been a humorous poem by Goethe – *Lili's Park*. Mendelssohn had written to his sister Fanny on November 16, 1830: 'I want to turn *Lili's Park* into a scherzo for a symphony'.

It is a movement of restrained and consummate grace which would not have been out of place in the gentle world of fairies and elves that Mendelssohn has so skilfully recreated in his music for *A Midsummer Night's Dream*. The scoring is immensely subtle: woodwind and horns are used with restraint to colour the strings' statement of the minuet, the first 20 bars of which are repeated. In the second part the scoring becomes much richer over the bed of strings, but trumpets and drums are still kept back in reserve.

The central *Trio* section (so-called because it was traditionally written in three-part harmony) opens with a soft fanfare (bassoons and horns) answered by a tripping upward phrase on violins. A repeat of the fanfare is then answered similarly by flute, and bassoons and horns complete their statement. This section is then repeated.

Now, but still with restraint (the dynamic marking is *mf* – medium loud), Mendelssohn brings in the trumpets and drums. For a few bars they support the fanfare, eventually playing it alone as, for a brief spell, tension heightens. A return to the beginning of the Trio section quickly dispels any unrest (note that violins and flute exchange places in their tripping phrase), and the minuet is restated intact. At the end, by way of a coda, the Trio

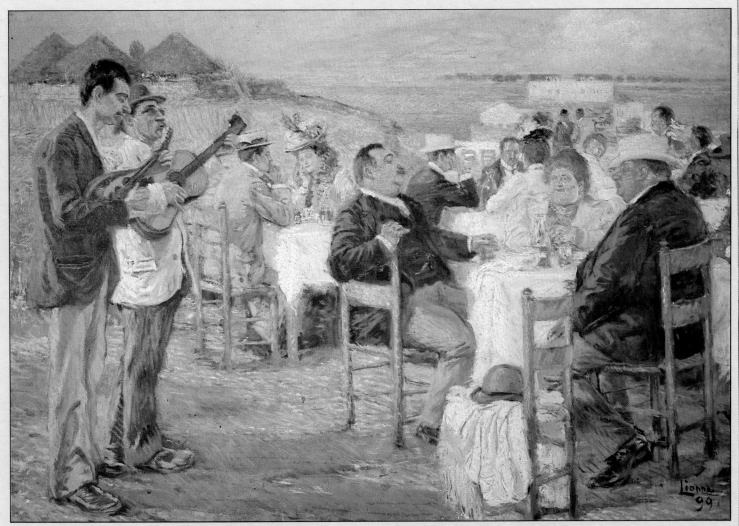

The 'Italian' Symphony as a whole is a vivid expression of Mendelssohn's impression of Italy and, in particular, the vitality of the Italian people (above).

section's fanfares are telescoped and combined with elements of the minuet.

Fourth movement – Presto – 'Saltarello'
Mendelssohn would appear to disagree with one aspect of the standard description of a *saltarello* – as a moderately rapid Italian dance involving jumping steps and written in triple metre – for this *'Presto'* tempo marking indicates something rather more boisterous and headlong.

Five decisive rhythmic chords bring the dancers to the centre of the floor. A burst of rhythmic strumming sets the tempo for the dance and the first dancer (represented by two flutes) begins 'lightly' (*leggiero*).

Example 5

Two clarinets soon join the dance, then, briefly and reluctantly, two bassoons. Excitement increases as more and more instruments are caught up in the swirl, bystanders stamping to reinforce the rhythm. Another *saltarello* tune soon arrives, switching back and forth between first and second violins and coloured by repeated trumpet *octaves* (notes which sound the same, though they are the bottom and top notes of an eight-note interval) and long descending phrases on oboe and clarinet.

For a moment the dance recedes, snatches of it still being heard clearly but as if from a distance. A running motif now appears and is given brief *fugato* (overlapping) treatment before capitulating to the *saltarello*. A sudden startling *unison* descent – in which the instruments sound the same notes – marks the beginning of the development section which, as the *saltarello* again fades, introduces a new dance: a *tarantella*:

Example 6

While the *saltarello* is peculiar to Rome, the *tarantella* comes from further south in Italy. It is a lively, fast-moving dance which was said to cure tarantism – the effects of the bite of the local spider, the tarantula. Many composers, including Weber, Chopin, Liszt and Rossini, have been inspired by its heady momentum to write a tarantella, more, of course, for the opportunity it provides for virtuosic display than for its therapeutic value. Many of Mendelssohn's characters, evidently, were in need of this cure, for one by one they join in as another and much more extended fugato develops. Hidden amongst its textures is an unmistakeable reference back to the cortège of the second movement: in the midst of life there is death. Could this be a semi-humorous warning about what would happen if a spider-bitten victim neglected to dance? It is far more likely an example of Mendelssohn's sheer composing exuberance.

Stray dancers on the edge of the *saltarello* gathering swirl close by and vanish again until, inevitably, the *saltarello* returns in full and the dancers mingle in a thrilling display of robust energy. Soon, however, they sink exhausted to the ground, the rhythms still pulsing through their brains. There is a rapid and violent crescendo and the Symphony is over.

LISTENER'S GUIDE
The art of the overture

In Mendelssohn's hands the overture became high art. Scenes of breezy summer gaiety, the dignity of a Spanish court and heaving stormy seas – all brilliantly evoked by his masterful music.

The overture in Mendelssohn's hands was essentially what later composers were to call a symphonic, or tone, poem. It was an impressionistic painting in music, usually portraying a natural scene, or catching the mood of a literary work. Although Mendelssohn was not the first composer to establish the overture as a self-contained work of this kind, he was still early enough in musical history to be a pioneer in this direction, providing an obvious guide to later composers, such as Brahms, Richard Strauss and Dvořák, as well as a considerable impetus to the Romantic movement in general.

The biggest impetus for the birth of

Romanticism in music was the composers' growing awareness of the literary world. In seeking 'pictorial' inspiration for music, they took account of the parallel efforts of artists and writers. It is not surprising that such large and influential figures as Goethe and Shakespeare were so important to the musical Romantic, for they supplied the vivid dramatic stories and the lyrical depths. Mendelssohn had no more opportunity than the rest of the world to hear most of Schubert's music, which was not fully re-discovered until the second half of the 19th century. But the comparatively few Schubert songs that became known in Mendelssohn's lifetime (1809–47), together with the flourishing Lieder (song) writing activities of lesser composers, must have been a strong influence on the composer who was a considerable song-writer himself.

Literary and musical influences

To Mendelssohn's table therefore came a feast of Shakespeare in the fashionable and accomplished translations by August Schlegel. (The composer was in fact connected to the great translator through his blue-stocking aunt, who married August Schlegel's brother.) As for Goethe, the gruff literary genius of the age, Mendelssohn had been able to visit the great man in 1821. They subsequently enjoyed a mutually approving relationship. Mendelssohn found Goethe 'very kind' and helpful, while Goethe was lavish in his praise of some of Mendelssohn's settings of his songs: a rare privilege as he was not a great praiser of musicians.

But probably the greatest practical influence on Mendelssohn was the operatic composer, Carl Maria von Weber, who visited Berlin in 1821. Mendelssohn went with his parents to the first performance of *Der Freischütz* and met the composer afterwards. Weber's Romantic innovations filled him with great enthusiasm and led him to write two or

The title page from Weber's **Der Freischütz.** *Mendelssohn's overtures were strongly influenced by Weber's colourful orchestrations.*

three immature operettas. But deeper than this went the effect of Weber's tight but colourful orchestration, which the young Mendelssohn used as his model. He found particular inspiration in Weber's *scherzos* (literally, 'a joke'). Mendelssohn was Weber's true heir and it is seen as a remarkable 'coincidence' that he wrote his *A Midsummer Night's Dream* overture just two months after Weber's death, using in it

a phrase that Weber had used in *Oberon* which was not heard publicly in Germany until a month or two later. Although Mendelssohn was said to have 'put the fairies to music', full credit must be given to Weber for having pioneered the path to fairyland.

There is a tendency at the moment to see Mendelssohn's rather delicate Romanticism, with its light though very imaginative use of the orchestra, as lacking the strong flavours of the committed Romantic. But here we must take account of his exact period. While Mendelssohn's symphonies still have one foot in the Classical period, the overtures move towards the Romantic era and make grateful use of literary associations to take this step into the future.

Programme notes

The Hebrides (Fingal's Cave), op. 26

In April 1829 Mendelssohn set off on a visit to London where his music was enthusiastically received and where he made many new friends. His close friend Karl Klingemann, a poet, had gone to England earlier and by now was living in Edinburgh, where he took Mendelssohn in July. Mendelssohn was greatly impressed by the Scottish scenery.

The friends travelled around, Mendelssohn sketching, Klingemann writing accompanying poems, and Mendelssohn conceived the ideas for a 'Scottish' symphony. They visited Sir Walter Scott at Abbotsford, suffered the

extremes of Scottish weather and went to the Inner Hebrides. Their destination was a strange natural phenomenon known as Fingal's Cave on the island of Staffa, a weird formation of pillar-like rocks that had been discovered in 1782 and named after a hero of Gaelic mythology. It had been visited by many famous people, including Queen Victoria. The friends endured a dreadful sea-trip from Oban to get there, but it was worth it. Klingemann described the cave as being 'like the inside of an immense organ, black and resonant, utterly without purpose, completely isolated'.

Mendelssohn wrote to tell his family about the visit and enclosed a sketch of the opening bars of the 'Hebrides' overture – 'In order to make you understand how extraordinarily the Hebrides affected me, I send you the following which came into my head there.' In fact, he had written the insistent little two-bar motif on the journey in perfect anticipation of what he was to see. It took him until December the following year to complete the overture but he felt dissatisfied with his first version. Following a performance in London in 1831 he thoroughly revised the score. It was not until November 1833, after three re-writes, that he was completely satisfied with the work.

The overture, scored for a normal classical orchestra without trombones, is fairly conventional in form but rich in imagination, a totally dramatic work that must have seemed very daring in its day and later proved an unavoidable model for any future portrayals of moving water. The

In spite of his sea-sickness Mendelssohn was so deeply impressed when he saw the black basalt cavern called Fingal's Cave (left), that he lost no time in sketching out the opening theme of what was to become **The Hebrides Overture.** *Ten years earlier the poet Keats had been similarly stirred: '. . . the sea' he wrote, 'is continually dashing there . . . For solemnity and grandeur it far surpasses the finest cathedrals.'*

first motif is a perfect evocation of wave movement, and is brought in right at the beginning by cellos, clarinets and bassoons. Its restless surge is to dominate

Example 1

throughout. This is allowed to work on our imagination, while a skilful touch in the scoring is the irregularly placed occasional drum-roll as an extra strong wave breaks on the rocks. The equally distinctive second subject in D major, with its upward movement, has more of the sea winds about it and it is offered by cellos, clarinets and bassoons. The waves increase as a third theme, a variation on the original motif, comes in *fortissimo* (very loudly), still in D, leading to a fanfare for horns and trumpets.

Mendelssohn develops an orchestral storm, beginning quietly with the original wave theme played by the lower strings against shimmering violins. There are frequent interruptions by woodwind and brass and the imagination is free to hear the cries of seabirds, even the bark of a seal. But, in fact, there is no actual attempt at realistic imitation; the whole effect is achieved simply by ceaseless movement, surges of sound, loud and then quiet, and quick changes of emphasis. The whole is restless and continually moving, the relentless pounding of the waves overlaid with all the smaller effects of sudden wisps of spray, gusts of wind and the bird-sounds. The music grows in intensity as the seas get stormier and there, with us right to the end, is that evocative theme suddenly dying away:

Example 2

The work was an instant success, even before Mendelssohn's final amendments. Wagner called the composer 'a first-class landscape painter'; and Brahms, as ever, wished that he would write something as good. It particularly won the hearts of the British who were grateful that such great music had been inspired by their island landscape. 'It brought', said one delighted writer, 'the perils of the sea straight into the concert hall'.

Ruy Blas, op. 95
As fitted his nature, the sensitive intellectual rather than the introspective Romantic, Mendelssohn was to find much of his inspiration in literary rather than

Understanding music: what is an overture?

Many overtures were composed for plays like **King Lear** *(above) but not as an accompaniment to a performance.*

The word 'overture' comes from the French *ouverture,* which means 'opening' and, in the 17th century, an overture was simply the piece that opened an opera or a similar event such as a ballet or oratorio. Italian operas, as well as French, had an opening piece, but they called it a *sinfonia* or *toccata.*

Typically, the French overture consisted simply of a slow opening section followed by a faster section to get the audience on their toes for the ensuing performance. The Italian overture which became predominant, however, could often be quite complex. In the 17th century, the Italian overture was just a single piece, starting fast, slowing down then speeding up again. But by the middle of the 18th century, these three sections had become separate movements.

For the composer, overtures and sinfonias often provided a much better opportunity to display their talents than the opera itself, which tended to be dictated by the strict demands of a programme. Naturally, they were tempted to put a lot of musical ideas into the overture. But audiences who had come to see an opera did not want a great weight of music before the performance and, by Mozart's time, the last two movements had been dropped – the movements only survived, and grew, in the form of symphonies.

Naturally, the overture would often be designed to set the mood for the performance that followed. A skilful composer would also weave some of the themes that were to appear in the opera into the overture – although overtures to later comic operas, such as those of Offenbach and Strauss, were merely medleys of the opera's main tunes. Nonetheless, despite their obvious links to the opera that followed, many of the better overtures could stand by themselves, and might be played in the concert hall long after the opera or play had been forgotten.

Overtures continued to be written for stage performances, and these are called *dramatic overtures.* But many composers, from the beginning of the 19th century onwards, became attracted by the idea of writing a similarly pictorial or dramatic piece for its own sake. One of the wonderful things about concert overtures was that the composer could let his imagination run wild and choose topics which could never be made into a work for the stage. Literary subjects, notably from Goethe and Shakespeare, were particularly popular.

In Mendelssohn, the concert overture reached its zenith and though many composers followed his lead, its popularity soon began to decline. By the 1870s, the overture form tended to be used only for rather lightweight medleys of folk tunes and only the rather conservative Brahms continued to write serious overtures.

natural sources. At least one of his literary experiences was to lead to a lasting masterpiece, but he was also capable of producing fine music for a work that did not particularly delight him – and to order. When he was asked to write some music, including an overture, for a charity performance of Victor Hugo's tragedy *Ruy Blas* (pronounced *rui blass*), staged in Leipzig in 1839, he was willing to oblige. He actually disliked the play, a violent and deeply pessimistic piece that found no real response in his nature. 'I intend to call it,' he jokingly told his mother, 'not the overture to *Ruy Blas,* but to the Theatrical Pension Fund.'

In *Ruy Blas* Hugo was painting a romanticized picture of the life and intrigues of the court of Charles II of Spain, taking considerable liberties with historical fact. 'The philosophical motive', Hugo explained, 'is a people aspiring to a higher state; its drama is the love of a servant for a queen.'

Ignoring this sort of thing, Mendelssohn wrote a shapely piece that belied his opinion of the play as 'detestable and more utterly beneath contempt than you could believe'. Asked for a romance and an overture by the Committee of the Leipzig Theatrical Pension Fund, he found at first only the will to write a song and asked to be excused from attempting the overture. The Committee knew their man, however, and wrote thanking him for the excellent romance while at the same time expressing the hope that he might be able to write an overture if given longer notice for next year's performance. Proud of his facility for musical creation, Mendelssohn replied by writing the overture in two days in between rehearsals.

By the time he came to write the *Ruy Blas* music the 'elfin' streak that his father urged him to abandon in favour of 'graver things' had been lost. (It was only to return in the pure serenity of the Violin Concerto of 1844.) Mendelssohn was now writing in the vein that seems closer to Berlioz and Liszt, composers he did not particularly admire. His lack of true response to Victor Hugo's work is to be found in the divergence of the overture from the path that the drama took, ending as it does on a fairly optimistic chord of C major, whereas the play's end is pure tragedy. The rest of the piece, melodramatic and full of foreboding in C minor, is thickly orchestrated with two flutes, two oboes, two clarinets, two bassoons, four horns, two trumpets and three trombones to help it towards a grand Berlioz-like sound.

There is no record of Mendelssohn himself explaining the connection between his music and the drama, and it is

In his overture **The Tale of the Fair Melusina,** *Mendelssohn depicts, with undulating watery figures, the legend of the spellbound heroine who, as a punishment, is turned into a mermaid for one day of each week.*

generally assumed that there is none, though one commentator, Sir George Macfarren, tied themes to persons with some conviction. What seems more likely is that Mendelssohn, writing in a state of 'amusing excitement', was far more concerned with the music than with its meaning. The overture starts with four slow and dignified bars that simply hint at the first theme, with a modified repeat. The principal theme is stated by the first violins and flutes with the other strings accompanying. This we may take to be a portrayal of the nature of *Ruy Blas*. The slow opening is repeated and now hints at the second theme, which is then stated by clarinet, bassoon and cellos – perhaps representing the queen. This is developed before a third theme, suggesting the raptures of love, is added. The various themes are repeated and woven together before a lively coda ends the overture.

The Tale of the Fair Melusina, op. 32

This overture was written in 1833 when Mendelssohn had become a well-known composer and travelling conductor, and was even considered by many to be the greatest European musician. He had gone to Düsseldorf to have a rest from his many activities in the hope of indulging undisturbed in some composition. He was inspired to write this overture after hearing a dull and ineffectual score for a libretto by the poet Franz Grillparzer based on a traditional legend.

In the story, Melusina is turned into a mermaid for one day of each week as a punishment for burying her father inside a mountain after he had mistreated her mother. Her husband Lusignan, whom she loves deeply, had promised that he would never investigate the mysterious weekly disappearance of his wife but, overcome by curiosity, he discovers her just on the point of turning into a mermaid. As a result she is doomed to stay in this shape for ever.

As usual, Mendelssohn did not try to tell his story too literally but rather to catch its mood and to put its themes into classical form. It is a warning to us not to read too much detail into other works (such as the 'Hebrides' overture) to learn that Mendelssohn was upset at Robert Schumann's vivid interpretation. The latter let his imagination run riot and spoke of 'those fables of the life deep down beneath the watery abyss, full of darting fish with golden scales, of pearls in open shells, of buried treasure, of emerald castles towering one above the other'. Originally Mendelssohn called the work *The Mermaid and the Knight* which gives it a much more earthy aspect.

Marked *allegro con moto* (lively and brisk) the overture begins with an undulating watery figure for clarinet:

Example 3

It is in this theme that many writers have seen the inspiration for Richard Wagner's *Rheingold* motif and the opening music of that opera. Here we take it to represent the fair Melusina herself. Mendelssohn develops her character, passing the theme from clarinet to flute and then to the strings. A chord from the woodwind heralds the second section which represents the bold knight Lusignan, now in a minor key. The actual second theme,

William Blake's Oberon, Titania and Puck with Fairies Dancing *(below) is a pictorial equivalent to Mendelssohn's musical vision of* A Midsummer Night's Dream.

introduced by the first violins with a backing of strings and clarinets, is of a distinctly amorous nature, and is developed with passion.

After presenting the two main characters, the true development begins. First, Melusina's theme is restated by the woodwind and then violins, which combines with Lusignan's theme, both becoming more and more passionate. A coda brings the work to a quiet, though rising ending.

There is no obvious adherence to the story, or any attempt to deal with the story's climax. It is simply an evocation, perhaps not even so much of the human element, as of the element that dominates the story – the sea. It was music for which Mendelssohn himself had a special affection and he was not pleased to have it overburdened with meaning.

A Midsummer Night's Dream, op. 21

This piece of music is probably more representative of the true Mendelssohn, or what we may like to think of as the true composer, than anything else he wrote. In the lovely summer of 1826 Mendelssohn first came into contact with Shakespeare's

The second half of Calm Sea and Prosperous Voyage *swells with optimism: the sails of the becalmed ship fill at last and send it shorewards in a freshening breeze.*

A Midsummer Night's Dream. He wrote to his sister Fanny: 'I've just finished two piano pieces in the summerhouse – and today or tomorrow I'm going to start dreaming midsummer night's dreams in it; a bit of sheer audacity!' He long remembered his discovery of Shakespeare and started to write his music, as he later told a friend, 'in a state of delirium'. Again, we must be careful not to read too much of the summer breezes into it, though a friend of the composer's tells us that Mendelssohn himself indicated the point where he had depicted a fly buzzing past. Nor is there any link with the play's story or characters; it is simply an evocation of its summer mood.

Mendelssohn showed his first score to his friend Alfred Marx, a brash young intellectual who had wormed his way into the family circle and was much disliked by Mendelssohn's father. He had a great hold on the young composer who took his advice very seriously until they quarrelled in 1839 after Mendelssohn criticized an oratorio that Marx had written. Thereafter he was a sworn enemy.

On this occasion Marx was pleased with the four opening chords of Mendelssohn's overture (which remained exactly as written) but found what followed 'merry, delightfully vivacious, altogether pleasant and altogether lovely' but not good enough to associate with Shakespeare.

Mendelssohn was deeply hurt and departed without a farewell. After a few days' sulky silence, Mendelssohn wrote to say that he had to agree and asked for Marx's help to put things right. Accepting his detailed criticisms he rewrote most of the work, retaining small parts here and there of which his friend had approved, and completing the final version in August.

In November the pianist Moscheles heard Felix and Fanny play a piano duet version and discovered a 'great though still youthful genius'. A private performance of the orchestrated work was given at the Mendelssohn house at Christmas. In February it was given its first public peformance in Stettin under the composer/conductor Karl Loewe. The concert also included Mendelssohn's A flat Concerto for two pianos (played by Loewe and Mendelssohn) and the first performance in that part of Europe of Beethoven's 9th Symphony in which Mendelssohn played among the first violins. The overture had a fine reception. 'The bloom of youth lies over it' was Robert Schumann's typically encouraging comment on the work.

The overture begins *allegro di molto* (very lively) in E Major with four long chords played by the woodwind followed by a quiet chord in E minor on the violins and violas. Then follows what has become known as the 'fairy music' given by the

violins with *pizzicato* viola accompaniment. An additional theme is added by the full orchestra. A melodious second theme in B major is started by the woodwind. This is followed by several smaller themes, which were later connected to characters in the play when Mendelssohn re-used them in the subsequent incidental music (written 17 years later in 1843). Most notable of these themes is the dance associated with Bottom's transformation with a lively imitation of an ass's bray – a touch liked by Marx who had persuaded Mendelssohn to retain it against his will. A rapid descending passage for cellos is Mendelssohn's response to the fly in the garden. The development is now based on the first theme, with a short coda. The whole ends with the four chords that started it.

It is difficult to ascertain how much of the music was intended to be associated with specific characters in the play when Mendelssohn first wrote the overture. But when he wrote the full incidental music, he made most skilful use of the overture's music in various guises.

Calm Sea and Prosperous Voyage, op. 27
The most purely literary of all Mendelssohn's overture inspirations, came from two short poems of Goethe's: 'Meeresstille' and 'Glückliche Fahrt'. The first portrays a profound stillness, the

ocean lying motionless, no breeze, a fearful silence, a monstrous waste – over which the anxious sailor gazes. To portray this Mendelssohn chooses an *adagio* (a slow movement) in D.

The introduction is based on a theme that appears later; the whole is a tone painting of the calmness suggested by the poem. There is little to explain except for the strange flute calls that end it – and these are beyond explanation unless we imagine the inevitable 'sea-bird'.

The second poem heralds the lifting of a sea-mist and a clear sky. A welcome breeze blows, the sails fill and the sailor bestirs himself. The waves divide and the long looked for land grows welcomingly near. In complete contrast, *molto allegro vivace* (very lively and vivacious), but still in D, Mendelssohn portrays the ship in action and its arrival in port. Lively passage work depicts the growing breeze with the opening theme from the first part now providing a basis for development. All is action with the noises of the ship represented in horn and trumpet calls. After a brief recapitulation, there is a short coda in which those ashore salute the ship's safe arrival and in the last three bars the vessel slides up to the quay.

Great interpreters

The London Symphony Orchestra
The orchestra was formed in 1904 through the breakaway of about 50 players from the old Queen's Hall Orchestra, and is now the oldest surviving London orchestra. From its inception it constituted itself as a self-governing organization, administered from within by a board elected from the players themselves.

Up until World War II the orchestra worked mainly through separate engagements and commissions from conductors, societies and other organizations, and so travelled extensively, touring abroad as early as 1906. In addition it played in many capacities in the musical activity of London. As well as this, it was first choice for all the Glyndebourne Festivals up to 1939.

During those inter-war years it was led at various times by most of the outstanding contemporary conductors, including Walter, Elgar, Nikisch, Richard Strauss, Beecham and Weingartner. It first recorded in 1920 and made many notable 78s.

World War II proved a time of great disruption, and although subsequently led by such fine conductors as Krips, Monteux and Kertesz, it wasn't until the later 1950s that, after a major internal upheaval, a marked improvement in playing standards was effected. Certainly, by the beginning of André Previn's association with the orchestra, its stock had risen enormously, and under his baton its reputation spread through both tours and a considerable body of important recordings.

The London Symphony is currently the resident orchestra for the new Barbican Arts Centre, with Claudio Abbado as principal conductor.

The British influence
It is particularly appropriate that the overtures for the *Midsummer Night's Dream* and the *Hebrides* should have become so popular in England and should be so frequently performed in London. After Goethe, the greatest German poet, Mendelssohn loved Shakespeare's poetry and those opening and closing sequences of his overture inspired by the play have a particular warmth in the string playing. Similarly, the flowering of the opening of the *Hebrides* overture shows his passion for Scottish scenery.

FURTHER LISTENING

Mendelssohn's orchestral and choral works

Twelve String Symphonies, op. posth
There is no doubt that Mendelssohn belongs to that select group of musical geniuses whose very earliest works show astonishing maturity and inventiveness. Mendelssohn wrote these short works between the ages of 12 and 14, showing striking resourcefulness in his scoring of the orchestra as well as a full mastery of form. Add to this the composer's characteristic verve and vitality, and you have music which is continually engaging and full of interest.

Elijah, op. 70 (1846)
Mendelssohn's most substantial choral work has always enjoyed great popularity with both the public and performers. As a whole, it perhaps lacks the sustained depth and drama of Bach and Handel at their most profound, but this should in no way be allowed to detract from the very high quality of much of the writing. Indeed, some commentators hold that a few of the composer's finest melodies are to be found within the solo arias.

Octet in E flat, op. 20 (1825)
Written at the age of 16, the Octet for Strings is to be counted amongst Mendelssohn's masterpieces. It is a work crammed full of sparkling invention while also exhibiting the composer's typical subtlety of craftsmanship. Its conception is tellingly original, down to the very choice of instruments, a combination virtually untried up to this work. Mendelssohn's natural congeniality and vigour are effortlessly communicated through melodic writing and harmonic invention of the highest order.

In the background

Scientists still argue whether our natures or our upbringing contribute most to our personalities, talents and behaviour. However, it is undeniable that we cannot help being affected to some extent by our surroundings. Great composers are no exception, and the following pages describe the historical background to Mendelssohn's life and the events that influenced and inspired him: the partnership of Queen Victoria and Prince Albert; and the advances in state education during the 19th century. Although Prince Albert was talented and well-meaning, he was never really popular among his wife's subjects – unlike his compatriot, Mendelssohn – perhaps because his manner was too formal and unbending and because he was seen to disapprove of the 'frivolous' pastimes enjoyed by the British. One movement he did approve of was the extension of education to the lower orders of society, a move which, with the extension of the franchise, was seen as increasingly necessary if disaffection amongst the working classes was to be avoided.

IN THE BACKGROUND

Queen Victoria and Prince Albert

Education for all

The modern image of Queen Victoria is of a solemn matriarch who disapproved of pleasure. However, during the early years of her reign while Prince Albert, her husband, was alive, the court was a centre of culture and enjoyment. Unlike Albert, Victoria was no intellectual, and she regarded the stirrings of democracy amongst her subjects as created by dangerous trouble-makers.

Albert, in contrast, was keen to promote the interests of the respectable 'industrious classes' – as in his support for the Society for the Improvement of the Labouring Classes – and saw the movements to extend the benefits of education outside the priviledged classes as a much-needed reform rather than as a danger to society.

IN THE BACKGROUND

'A model for the nation'

Despite demanding public roles, Victoria and Albert enjoyed an idyllic family life and were at one with their subjects in their enthusiasm for, among other things, Felix Mendelssohn's delightful music.

The term 'Victorian' has come to mean all things proper and restrained, heavy with solemnity and status. But Queen Victoria, in her early years at least, was not like that at all. When she married her distant cousin, Prince Albert of Saxe-Coburg-Gotha (a small German duchy), she married for love. To the 20-year-old Queen, Albert was an incredibly handsome and charming, even 'incomparable', man. She felt a deep physical passion for him, which she expressed quite openly in her letters, and though he was a rather more reserved person, he was totally dedicated to her.

They had many things in common, not the least of which was a love of family life that was partly due to the fact that they had both endured scandal and disruption in their own childhoods. Albert never saw his mother after the age of five when the Princess Louise of Saxe-Coburg-Gotha ran off with another man, and Victoria's father had died when she was a baby. Mindful of Albert's wayward mother and of Victoria's two shocking uncles – George IV and William IV – the royal couple shared a desire, almost raised to a sacred obligation, to set new standards of respectability.

A model family

In the early years of their idyllic marriage Victoria and Albert set about initiating an exemplary style of royal living. Despite a stifling emphasis on etiquette and formality on public occasions, daily family life was

Though still girlish and fun-loving, the 20-year-old Victoria (far left) had clear ideas about marriage. It had to be a love match and her partner had to come up to high standards of male beauty.

Albert might have been tailor-made: he fulfilled all of the Queen's hopes with his 'beautiful blue eyes, an exquisite nose, & such a pretty mouth with delicate moustachios & slight but very slight whiskers'. She was happy to propose (left) in October 1839, and when he accepted they immediately fell into each other's arms. They were married in February 1840 (below) and within a year the first of their many children, Princess 'Vicky', was born.

The 'new and much admired' royal 'pear' (above).
Victoria and Albert were exemplary newly-weds.

characterized by a refreshing informality. An artist engaged to paint frescoes at Buckingham Palace observed how, after their diplomatic and political work, the young couple would stroll out into the grounds, 'evidently delighted to get away from the bustle of the world to enjoy each other's society in the solitude of the garden . . . Here too the royal children are brought out by the nurses, and the whole arrangement seems like real domestic pleasure'. There is no doubt that the royal household was a very happy one. Victoria never disguised her distaste for tiny babies and she confessed that too many pregnancies – she had nine children in 17 years – had made her 'so worn out' and 'so miserable', but she was a devoted mother.

Despite her distaste for childbearing, a process she always referred to with typical delicacy as *die Schattenseite* (the shadow-side) of marriage, Victoria was lucky in that she was as vigorously healthy as she was fertile. Her first baby was born three weeks prematurely and though the immediate reaction was one of disappointment at the failure to produce an heir, this was the only blot on an otherwise perfect birth. 'Oh Madam,' said the doctor in charge, 'it is a princess.' 'Never mind', was the matter-of-fact Queen's reply, 'the next one will be a prince.' After her 12-hour labour she found herself in no pain whatsoever and she had a good appetite. 'Dearest Albert hardly left me at all and was the greatest comfort and support.' In view of the fact that even until recently fathers were kept well away from the labour room, Prince Albert's involvement is all the more surprising, and touching. During all of Victoria's

Prince Albert, like his wife, was also a fond and conscientious parent. He introduced decorated 'German' trees as an element in the royal family's Christmas. The innovation was a congenial reminder of the Prince Consort's foreign-ness and, as this Victorian Christmas card's theme shows, the custom soon caught on in Britain and elsewhere.

Family life at Windsor (above). Victoria and Albert saw a great deal more of their nine children than many other aristocratic Victorian parents, but they relished their evenings alone together. The Queen disliked small babies, but she was a loving mother of her children as they grew beyond the 'frog-like' stage. Her own sketches, Prince Arthur (left) and Princess Beatrice (far left), reveal her absorption with them. Beatrice was born with the help of 'soothing, quieting and delightful' chloroform, a fact that helped to make the use of anaesthetics in childbirth popular.

confinements he alone lifted her from her bed to her sofa and for this purpose he would come instantly from any part of Windsor Castle.

Albert was, moreover, a paragon of Victorian fatherliness. Though strict and rather pompous in his expectations, he was never unapproachable. The royal children were seen and very much heard, and saw their parents far more than many aristocratic children of the day. One lady-in-waiting observed that 'the beloved parents have nothing so much at heart as the right training of these precious children.'

Although Albert could not, as a foreigner and a consort, take part in the monarchy's constitutional role, he certainly did what he could to run Victoria's household well. He saved thousands of pounds by abolishing many outdated or downright wasteful customs. The Queen had never seen a fire in the dining room at Windsor Castle, for example, because according to old court rules the Lord Steward had to lay the fire, and the Lord Chamberlain had to light it. As a result, she had always eaten in the cold. This was the sort of thing Albert put a stop to.

Prince Albert's management of the household economy included also the running of the farm and estates at Windsor and elsewhere. He was quick to implement the most modern techniques and was much admired as a resourceful and efficient farmer. All the bulls were named after members of the royal family – one was even named Fitzclarance after an illegitimate son of William IV – and this touch indicates that Albert was not, contrary to contemporary opinion, entirely lacking in a sense of humour.

'Home sweet home'

In his role as the ideal husband and father Albert also devoted a great deal of energy to the various royal family homes: first Osborne, on the Isle of Wight, and later Balmoral in Scotland. Victoria and Albert found Windsor Castle too oppressively grand, but Osborne was relatively 'cosy'. This seaside house was purchased in 1845 and rebuilt according to the royal couple's, or rather Albert's, specifications. Here was a purpose-built setting for an idyllic family life. An entire Swiss cottage was erected in the grounds for the children to play in and their father regularly joined them in hide-and-seek games in the surrounding woodland, even demonstrating the art of turning somersaults in the haystacks – undoubtedly to the delight of the royal children.

Throughout Osborne House the entwined initials V

and A still speak of that happy Victorian marriage – everywhere, that is, except over the smoking-room door, whose function as a male sanctum is indicated by a single A. The interiors at Osborne can still be seen. They are heavy, ornate and loaded with bric-à-brac: every surface is covered by paintings and family portraits, or littered by items such as hand-painted china ornaments and replicas, cast in silver or bronze, of dead family pets. Osborne was an enormous version of the kind of home that every respectable middle-class family aspired to create. Indeed the Queen was also very typical of her age in her taste for collecting.

This love of material things had started early in her life with a collection of dolls, perhaps begun as a consoling substitute for brothers and sisters. In every establishment Victoria owned there were boxes and cupboards filled to capacity with china plate, silver objects and clothing, as well as accessories for every conceivable occasion. Later in life she took to having every room setting photographed, and every object catalogued, and in her widowhood she would enjoy thumbing through these volumes, as if to ensure that the past with all its mementoes would never slip away.

Almost everything the royal family did, their respectable subjects imitated – and so Scotland and all things Scottish did well out of Albert and Victoria's love for the Highlands. While Osborne served well as a family home, it was still near London. But Scotland was less accessible, and there Victoria and Albert could more definitely escape the cares of state. They welcomed the seemingly relaxed attitude of the Scots to royalty and the unpretentious, wholesome atmosphere of the Highlands. The growth of the railway system greatly enhanced the possibility of getting away from it all. Victoria was much impressed by the speed and privacy that trains offered, and first used a train to travel from London to Windsor in 1842. She later availed herself of her own private carriage, built in 1869, to transplant her to Balmoral, the chosen Scottish base, overnight. Victoria and Albert had the castle rebuilt – complete with towers, castellated gables and turrets – in 1853, in order to have space for their large family and the inevitable visits of government ministers.

Balmoral was situated amid a stunningly romantic landscape and its interior was a positive riot of colour, for 'tartanitis' was a royal ailment. Lord Rosebery was heard to comment that he thought the drawing room at Osborne was the ugliest place he had ever seen until he saw the equivalent at Balmoral. 'Here everything is Scotch – the curtains, the carpets, the furniture, are all different plaids, and the thistles are in such abundance that they would rejoice the heart of a donkey if they happened to look like his favourite repast, which they don't. I am told it is *de rigueur* to clothe oneself in tweed directly.' But Lord Rosebery was in a minority. The royal mania for all things Scottish was sufficient to stimulate a boom for manufacturers of tweed and tartan, internationally as well as nationally.

As might be guessed, the Queen and the children learned Scottish dancing; while Albert engaged in 'manly' pursuits such as deer-stalking. Sometimes the royal couple went out into the Highlands for picnics, or travelled incognito, with perhaps just a couple of attendants. In her journal the Queen recorded her

Albert reformed the administration of the royal household with such economizing zeal that Osborne on the Isle of Wight (right) and Balmoral (below right) were bought out of the resulting savings. Purchased in 1845, Osborne was rebuilt as a family holiday home and was easily accessible by rail. Victoria and Albert enjoyed travelling by train and are shown (below) in their luxurious private saloon car with King Louis-Philippe of France.

BBC Hulton Picture Library

for want of trying on Albert's part, and the country had much to be grateful for. Victoria was almost absurdly ignorant of her people and she had very little knowledge of the great changes being brought about by the industrial revolution. She fretted about the increasing number of working-class people swelling the new cities of her realm. During her lifetime the vote was gradually extended so that by 1867 some working-class men were enfranchised, but the Queen continued to regard democrats and socialists as dangerous trouble-makers. She herself had started as a Whig, under the influence of Lord Melbourne, but in old age, charmed by Disraeli, she preferred the Conservatives.

But Albert was more realistic and more aware of the adjustments that great social and economic changes required in the monarchy's role and style. The Prince's interest in the 'industrious classes' turned Victoria's thoughts more charitably in their direction and she helped him with speeches to such worthy bodies as the Society for the Improvement of the Labouring Classes. Albert also saw to it that the Queen played an important part, above the whirl of electoral politics, in promoting industry and influencing foreign attitudes towards Britain. The success of the Great Exhibition of 1851 was largely due to Albert's vision and his hard work in organizing it. But his openness to modern developments in technology and the arts still militated against spontaneous popularity. The shrewd King Leopold of Belgium, Victoria's uncle and one of her father-figures, was provoked to warn his niece about the undesirability of Albert's interests. 'These dealings with artists, for instance, require great prudence. They

ecstatic delight in open-air outings and rough suppers in country inns, although often the party would be recognized and sent on its way with a cheer.

The Queen's own account of her Highland life, *Leaves from a Journal of our Life in the Highlands,* was subsequently (1868) published. Illustrated with her own sketches and bound in moss-green covers adorned with golden antlers, it sold 20,000 copies at once and quickly went through several editions. Some foreign and domestic critics groaned at Victoria's childlike style, while others, such as the astute Prime Minister Disraeli (himself an accomplished novelist) saw it as a chance for rank flattery – he gratified the Queen's ego by addressing her as 'We authors . . .' But the general public were, as ever, drawn to the personality of the Queen, so open, honest and heart-warming.

Albert's image
With the exception of the period when she was the secluded 'Widow of Windsor', Victoria was extremely popular as a monarch and a personality. But though Albert was respected he was never regarded with the same affection. His prowess in horse-riding and shooting could not make up for the fact that he was a very serious, high-minded person. The English aristocracy was extremely suspicious of his intellectual interests and the people suspected him as a 'foreigner'. It was even suggested, at the time of the Crimean War, that Albert was involved in handing over state secrets to Russia, and two London newspapers actually reported that the poor man had been accused of high treason and sent to the Tower.

Victoria, who declared that her husband 'always *fascinates* wherever he goes', was offended all her life by the fact that Albert never seemed to be accepted or loved freely by the populace and the court. It was not

BBC Hulton Picture Library

are acquainted with all classes of society, and for that very reason are dangerous.' If Albert had been stupid, flirtatious and lazy, he might have been adored and appreciated by many more than his wife.

In Victoria's case, Leopold's warning was not necessary: she quite liked to sing and to play the piano, but she avoided the company of intellectuals and once said that she never felt quite at ease when reading a novel. She enjoyed playing cards, loved charades, riddles, or games of that sort, and simply adored dancing. Luckily Albert enjoyed this too, and the Queen was blessed with a husband with whom she could waltz away – in total propriety! Her prowess as a dancer was always remarked on, and she continued to be lively until well into her 40s. Although she disapproved of heavy drinking, she always attended the servants' balls at Balmoral. When these reached the wildest stage, with bodies falling under the table, Victoria would simply pretend that nothing out of the ordinary was happening.

She could take the art of ignoring the awkward to extraodinary lengths. Her servant-companion of later years, the gillie John Brown, was notorious for his intake of Scotch. When on one occasion he fell to the ground in a drunken stupor, Queen Victoria maintained that she had felt a 'slight earthquake shock'. But where she felt it necessary she would observe the strictest rules. She hated smoking – so much so that, at Windsor Castle, guests of high rank would be seen lying on the floor of their bedrooms, in pyjamas, blowing the smoke up the chimneys in order to avoid detection.

A 'wonderful genius'

In addition to their shared love of their chidren, country life and dancing, Victoria and Albert both enjoyed music. The Queen had a beautiful singing voice, but her tastes were fairly low-brow. She preferred the Italian operas and light pieces by Rossini to choral works by Handel. But Prince Albert had been tutored in a rather more rigorous way and he liked to play Bach at the organ. Losing himself in his world of music, seated at the organ at Windsor Castle, was one of the ways in which he consoled himself in the early years of his marriage for the loss of his country, his family and his friends. (For political reasons he was not allowed to bring any close retinue with him to his

marital home in England.)

It was not surprising, therefore, that Felix Mendelssohn – a German, handsome, a perfect gentleman, and the creator of comfortable, homelike music – suited the royal tastes entirely. Mendelssohn himself was spiritually at home in England. He spoke the language well and was warmed by the public's enthusiasm for his music. His first important work was based on Shakespeare *(A Midsummer Night's Dream Overture)*; his Scottish Symphony was dedicated to Queen Victoria, and the *Hebrides Overture* (Fingal's Cave) has always remained one of the most popular pieces of his work in Britain.

Mendelssohn first met the Queen and Prince Albert five years after their marriage. He played for the Prince and the Queen, Albert then played a chorale for him and Victoria sang one of his songs. The composer then

Albert plays to a thoughtful Mendelssohn and an enchanted Victoria (right). Victoria and Albert were sincere Mendelssohn fans and the composer was twice 'summoned' to meet them at Buckingham Palace. The Queen, he wrote to his mother, 'is gentle, courteous and gracious. She speaks good German and knows my music well'.

Infatuated with Highland life, Victoria and Albert stimulated a great vogue for all things Scottish. The whole family, including the Queen, learned 'Scotch reels' (above left); the royal children were dressed in 'Highland things'; while Albert, with the help of an intimidatingly huge dictionary, applied himself with typical diligence to the learning of Gaelic.

entranced his royal audience by improvising on two themes, which he asked them to suggest: Rule Britannia and the Austrian National anthem. Mendelssohn wove these two into a little piece and somehow managed to blend in the themes from the songs that Victoria had sung, thus demonstrating his genius and his charm. In a letter home to his mother after the event, Mendelssohn was happy to say that the pleasure and attentiveness of Victoria and Albert 'put me in better humour than usual when I improvise for an audience'.

The composer visited the court again two years later. His many happy experiences in the country moved him to give the first public performance of his oratorio, *Elijah,* to open the Birmingham Music Festival in 1846. Oratorios had been favourite works in England since the time of Handel and they suited the high religious feeling of the Victorians. Mendelssohn came to England to supervise rehearsals, and again to conduct the work on subsequent occasions. Victoria and Albert attended the second London performance, and invited the composer to perform at Buckingham Palace. The Queen also

attended a concert with the London Philharmonic, at which Mendelssohn played a Beethoven concerto. In her typically simple style, she noted in her journal:

It was so full of feeling and soul & his touch was wonderful. He played entirely by heart, which, when doing so with the orchestra must be most difficult. He is a wonderful genius & is deservedly an amazing favourite here . . .

'Mr Mendelssohn's' popularity with the royal family was reflected in the fact that in 1858 the Queen's eldest daughter left her marriage ceremony to the strains of his Wedding March and as an old lady Victoria is said to have boasted that the charming composer had 'taught' her singing. The Queen's claim was somewhat exaggerated, but was a tribute to the success of her meetings with the composer.

The master in the house
On many matters of taste Victoria and Albert were at one with their middle-class subjects, but in one area in particular their marriage had a profound influence. Though Victoria was the Queen, Albert was most

From Balmoral Victoria and Albert enjoyed trips to local beauty spots, which climaxed with elaborate picnics. But the trip to Cairn Lochan in 1861 (above) was the last such outing to include the Prince Consort, who died in the same year.

definitely the head of their family. While Victoria may have started out married life full of enthusiasm and a certain tolerance, she gradually became more severe and disapproving of impropriety. No divorced woman could enter the court, and no re-married widow either. She also abdicated a great deal of personal freedom, deferring to Albert on many issues, public and private, during their married life. Given that she was single when she acceded to the throne and showed remarkable agility then in handling her own affairs, this passive attitude must have been inculcated by Albert. She once wrote to King Leopold, 'We women are not *made* for governing – and if we are good women, we must dislike these masculine occupations.' And dislike them she did.

But it would be wrong to form the impression that Albert and Victoria were a perfectly bourgeois royal family. This was not the case. From the start they both shared a deep belief in the importance of the monarchy. Even if their family life was a model to lesser folk, Victoria and Albert were perfectly matched in their high aspirations and regal self-consciousness. This quality was evident on Victoria's visit to France in 1855 (she was the first British monarch for several generations to travel abroad). Standing alongside that paragon of French chic, the new Empress Eugénie, the English queen was, as usual, unfashionably attired – Albert was no help at all in this respect. Some French dignitaries were amused by Victoria's outfit. She wore an enormous bonnet and a dress patterned with vivid geraniums that would have done credit to a window-box. A crude green parasol shielded her and she carried a huge handbag embroidered with a white poodle, which had been a present from one of her daughters. But despite these ludricous accessories, and the unfavourable contrast between her tiny, stout

figure and that of the slender, pace-setting Empress Eugénie, there was no doubt in the Parisian public's mind as to Victoria's status. An almost serene regal composure attended her down to the last detail.

In 1861 Prince Albert died, quite suddenly, of typhoid. He was only 42 and Victoria was overwhelmed by grief. Now she was on her own as the widowed head of a large, and still young, family and the occupant of a role that gave few allowances for such distress. She suffered from the temporary physiological changes that modern drugs can alleviate. She felt cold and she lost weight; she could hardly walk and she suffered from dreadful headaches. Together her 'symptoms' added up to what might be described, and better understood, today as a nervous breakdown. For five years she became the secluded, and therefore unpopular 'Widow of Windsor', devoting her time to the commemoration of her husband in every conceivable way. Even so, the length of her mourning period, and the somewhat morbid expressions of it, were not so outlandish in an age when small children were often dressed in black after the death of a remote relative. The problem was that Victoria had an 'outside' duty to perform – people expected the royal show to go on.

When she finally emerged, in 1866, she had a new man, literally, to lean upon – Her Majesty's Highland Servant John Brown – and his platonic, supportive presence helped her back into her public position as the Queen of England. Then, she seemed indestructible. Her 50th anniversary in 1887 marked the high tide of her popularity, and in 1897 the Diamond Jubilee – for the longest reigning English monarch – was equally magnificent. It was 1901, 40 years after the death of her 'dear Angel', before she was laid to rest alongside Albert at Frogmore.

Clad in deepest mourning, Victoria and Princess Alice sit despondently around a bust of Albert. The Queen was desolated by his early death: 'My life as a happy one has ended. The world has gone for me.' In her immense grief she devoted herself to commemorating him in every possible way. She even had a plaque erected on the spot where he had shot his last stag and for 40 years fresh clothes continued to be laid out in his room every evening, together with hot water and a clean towel.

IN THE BACKGROUND

'Willingly to school'

*As the son of wealthy parents Mendelssohn had an
expensive private education, but he lived at a time
when a rudimentary schooling was beginning to
be seen as a right as well as a privilege.*

In the first half of the 19th century educational
standards reflected little credit on European civilization. The populations of revolutionary, rationalist
France and industrially mighty Britain were 40 to 50
per cent illiterate, while some of the peoples who
made up the Austrian Empire rivalled the Spaniards
and Portuguese in their claim to almost total
illiteracy. Only the Germans, Scandinavians, Swiss
and Dutch made successful efforts to teach reading
and writing at all levels of society. This contrast
reflected a divergence of national attitudes. British

governments tended to leave learning to private
enterprise (England and Wales only acquired a state
system of primary education in 1870). The Prussians,
however, delighted in the extension of state
authority into any field, including that of education,
and their pioneering schooling system earned the
admiration of Europe.

Classics and grammar

In Germany the most common way of becoming
eligible for university education was to endure the

*Before the introduction
of mass education in
the 19th century, most
ordinary people could
neither read nor write.
As illiterates, they often
relied on the services of
travelling newsreaders
(below), equipped with
visual aids.*

Archiv für Kunst und Geschichte

William Stewart 'Interior of an Academy'. Yale Center for British Art.

Friedrich Froebel (1782–1852) was a German educational reformer whose interest in the needs of pre-school children led him to found the first kindergartens (left).

full rigour of 13 years at a classical grammar school (*Gymnasium*). Because this secondary education was not free, it was largely limited to the sons of the upper classes, and some artisans and small tradesmen. Indeed, as has always been the case, many families struggled to pay for the secondary education of their sons. (Mendelssohn's tutor Zelter spent some years at the *Gymnasium* although he was only the son of a mason.) But those who could not afford the university-orientated grammar school had a compulsory period of attendance at primary school between the ages of six and fourteen, where a very basic education was provided. Once a pupil reached the *Gymnasium* he usually faced a sturdy attempt to deny him anything approaching a modern education. This approach had its roots in the well-meaning and high-minded reforms introduced by Wilhelm von Humboldt, Prussian Minister of Education in the second decade of the 19th century. Impeccably liberal, von Humboldt felt that a study of Ancient Greek civilization would encourage democratic ideals among young Germans.

As the teachers were themselves products of classical education they mounted a stout resistance to the introduction of more practical subjects such as modern languages or mathematics. This obsession with the classics was not a uniquely German phenomenon, however. Britain's rather curiously termed 'public' schools, most of which were either

In village primary schools (below) only the four R's – reading, writing, 'rithmetic and religion – were generally taught. The great emphasis on classical studies (left) began at secondary school, which only a minority attended.

founded or reformed in the 19th century under the influence of Thomas Arnold of Rugby School, shared this concentration. Dr Arnold himself was earnest, god-fearing and utterly steeped in the classics. In the 1830s he reformed his school from being a violent, rough-and-tumble place like the other public schools of its day (including Eton), into a centre of 'really Christian education'. Since his interest was in a moral, as opposed to a useful or career-orientated education, physical science was not taught at the new-style Rugby. The boys' main studies were the dead languages of Greece and Rome. 'Rather than have physical science the principal thing in my son's mind,' Dr Arnold confidently declared, 'I would gladly have him think that the sun went round the earth, and that the stars were so many spangles set in the bright blue firmament. Surely the one thing needful for a Christian and an Englishman to study is Christian and moral and political philosophy.' And most of the parents of young 'gentlemen' agreed heartily with such sentiments.

Even when the iron grip of classics began to loosen towards the middle of the century alternatives were quickly killed off by the average teacher's genius for making schoolwork dull. In this way enthusiasm for natural history as a subject would soon be choked when the pupil discovered that learning the subject consisted solely in learning by rote the names of all 160 bones of the human body. Classics, too, must have suffered from this approach although there were, no doubt, some teachers who tried to communicate their love for Virgil's or Homer's verses to their pupils. For most however, schooling was merely a deadening process of acquiring the credentials necessary for a respectable lifestyle.

The education of girls

If the *Gymnasium's* rough and rather unintellectual atmosphere made it unsuitable for sensitive boys such as Felix Mendelssohn, it was also unattainable

Rugby School (above). Under the influence of the dynamic Dr Arnold, it was organized to produce 'Christians, gentlemen and scholars, in that order'. In keeping with this low emphasis on intellectual ability, the curriculum was dull, being mainly devoted to the classics and religion. But games, especially the sport that derived its name from the school, were another vital component of the English public schoolboy's experience.

for their sisters. It is not unfair to say that most girls were educated simply to fulfil the role expected of them as suitable marriage partners. That working women should be basically educated was not in dispute and the daughters of poor people were as well schooled as their male equivalents. But the middle classes had very limited ideas as to the sort of woman they considered ideal and they educated their daughters accordingly. The more liberal parents (and those who could afford it) thought that a woman should have social graces and cultivated any aptitude for singing, music or drawing. The majority, however, found female learning of any sort an uncomfortable threat to masculine predominance.

Family life was something of a conservative German cult and it relied to a great extent on an idealized, docile and domesticated wife and mother. Because of the shortage of job opportunities for middle-class German men before 1850 (there were, of course, virtually no jobs for respectable 'ladies'), they were often middle aged before they were financially secure enough to marry. As a result, men tended to seek wives ten or twenty years younger than themselves and they maintained something of a father-daughter relationship with them. The last thing they needed was an educated wife whose cleverness might have damaged their self-esteem. The English novelist, George Eliot, wrote sarcastically on this theme: 'First comes French, then the piano, that she shall be able to amuse and soothe her husband, and lastly a thorough acquaintance with the principles of household economy in its highest and most aesthetic sense, including the art of knitting purses.'

To keep pace with the demand for docile housewives, girls' schools tended to offer a rather limited academic curriculum, though there were a few more liberal fathers for whom this was not enough.

Abraham Mendelssohn recognized that his elder daughter Fanny had a strong musical talent and he encouraged this just as he encouraged that of Felix; yet there were subtle differences of emphasis between the education of the two. Felix was expected to achieve academic distinction and, if possible, to proceed to university so that much

Archiv für Kunst und Geschichte

© Midsummer Books Ltd.

This Victorian painting of a boy struggling with his homework inadvertently illustrates the difference between the education of boys and girls in the 19th century. His sister is still half-absorbed in her sewing.

attention was paid to his classical studies. Fanny, on the other hand, was not urged on in the same way and was excused Greek, which Felix would have had to study by himself if he had not persuaded his younger sister Rebekka to keep him company. The point was that there was absolutely no chance of Fanny proceeding to higher education because this was, effectively, closed to women.

There was the case of Dorothea, daughter of Professor Schlozer at Gottingen, who took her doctorate in 1787 at the age of 17, but she was unique and her father was widely considered to be eccentric (as he was). Even the most liberal of the age's leading intellectuals were hostile to poor Dorothea's achievement and Schiller termed it a 'farce' in a letter to Goethe, who proclaimed, 'Let women learn early to serve, as is their destiny.' It was not until 1894 that the first grammar school for girls was opened in Germany and German universities only began to open their doors to women after 1901.

Home tuition

The Mendelssohn children had a far richer and more varied education than any meted out in the *Gymnasium* because they were privately tutored. For a minority of the rich this sort of arrangement was

While her charges divert themselves, this governess (left) looks lonely and pale. The painting offers an all too real image of the private tutor's role in wealthy homes.

Students at Heidelberg University (right) live it up. In the 19th century universities were seen as places of residence and discussion rather than centres for training and research. If they had any practical aim, it was to produce social leaders.

The new University of Berlin (above), started after 1806, became the model of most German universities, which in turn were to influence the pattern of modern academic institutions all over the world.

Eyres were to find more public roles as teachers within the expanding primary education systems of Europe. Although poorly paid, the schoolmistress became a new kind of heroine, a central figure in small villages where children were, often for the first time, acquiring a basic education.

Obviously, the quality of home tuition depended to a great extent on the individual family's means. But the fact that such education was organized within homes did not mean that life was any more comfortable for the pupils because many private tutors were just as ferociously keen on discipline as their counterparts in the *Gymnasium* and public school. It seems to have been a fairly well accepted principle, for example, that a single moment's idleness in a child was intolerable. A small girl sitting with her hands upon her lap would be told to cut a hole in her pinafore and mend it rather than do nothing. Every moment not spent at academic study had to be constructively used. Thus reading, drawing, physical exercises, music and dancing were acceptable alternatives to mental learning, but free or spontaneous forms of play were not. In running this sort of regime, private tutors usually had the full support of their employers, the parents, who preferred their children to be seen and not heard.

Mendelssohn's parents were an exceptional couple, however. Abraham Mendelssohn was very rich indeed, and he and his wife Lea were highly cultured and took great pleasure in the company of the distinguished artists and thinkers who thronged Lea's salon. The result of this wealth and these connections with the intellectual aristocracy of Germany was that the children had the best tutors and hardly lacked for stimulating company. Felix's piano tutor was Ludwig Berger, his violin teacher was Eduard Rietz and he was taught harmony, counterpoint and composition by Karl Friedrich Zelter – not for him a single, general-purpose music teacher. Also, a cultivated and interested mother contributed a great deal to the early educational achievements of children.

But despite his excellent education, Felix Mendelssohn was at a slight disadvantage compared with boys who had gone through the *Gymnasium* when it came to entering university. Simply completing attendance at the *Gymnasium* and returning a satisfactory record for each year's study was the usual way into university. But for those who might have attained university standard through private education, there had to be some proof of academic qualification. As usual, competence in the classics was the yardstick by which an aspiring undergraduate was judged. The idea was to produce a thesis or some example of the student's work which was creditable enough to be recognized as proof of his fitness to attend university. In the case of Felix Mendelssohn his tutor Dr Karl Wilhelm Ludwig Heyse urged him to produce a translation of the Latin poet Terence's *Andria* in the metre of the original. This proved quite acceptable and Felix matriculated at Berlin University in May 1827.

normal. Indeed the popular image of the abused governess – most famously expressed in Charlotte Brontë's *Jane Eyre* – reflects the realities of these private arrangements. In fact governessing was one of the few means of self-support available to poor but well-bred young women, who frequently suffered from their ambiguous status – half-servants, half members of the family – in upper-class households. Gradually, however, many of these isolated Jane

The cadet school

As far as entry to university was concerned the *Gymnasium* and private education had the same end in view but there was one peculiarly German type of schooling – the cadet school – which had a very different objective. There were eight cadet schools in Prussia and one each in Saxony and Bavaria. They provided free or assisted schooling for

Archiv für Kunst und Geschichte

Wilhelm von Humboldt (left) was an enlightened administrator and the prime mover behind the educational progress in early 19th-century Prussia.

Bildarchiv Preussischer Kulturbesitz

G. W. F. Hegel (right) was the intellectual star of Berlin University. Among his students were Mendelssohn, Moltke and Karl Marx, whose political philosophy owed much to Hegel's ideas.

the sons of officers and poor noblemen, and their purpose was to turn out a military élite to officer the army. In terms of austerity and discipline, as well as the professional and social advantages they conferred in later life, they bore a marked resemblance to British public schools. Although the Prussian army later became rather famously uninterested in intellectual pursuits, this was not the case in the early 19th century when many young officers capitalized on the excellent education provided at the cadet schools. Bismarck's brilliant general, Helmut von Moltke, attended lectures at Berlin University, where he claimed that half of the audience were young officers like himself. Born some nine years before Mendelssohn, Moltke was nearly a contemporary and might well have been haunting the lecture halls of Berlin at the same time. In addition to leaving him with this taste for academic diversions, Moltke's cadet school equipped him with an excellent knowledge of English.

University life

In Mendelssohn and Moltke's day Berlin University was a fairly new creation, having been founded between 1806 and 1810 as part of Wilhelm von Humboldt's educational reforms and also as a part of the Prussian revival after the shock of defeat by the French at the Battle of Jena (1806). A friend of Goethe and Schiller, Wilhelm von Humboldt set up Berlin University with typically high-minded intentions: 'the end of man, or that which is prescribed by the eternal or immutable dictates of reason, and not suggested by vague and transient desires, is the highest and most harmonious development of his powers to a complete and consistent whole'. Despite the presence at Berlin of intellectual giants such as the great philosopher Hegel and Humboldt's own brother, the scientist and explorer Alexander von Humboldt, most of the students did not achieve this 'highest and most harmonious development'. Instead, they experienced little more than a rounding-off of the education they had already received at secondary school.

University students were a tiny minority in the 19th century. In the whole of mid-century Europe (including Britain) there were only about 40,000 students in all. Even so, this small élite was a growing minority, and beginning to become a politically significant one – in the revolutions of 1848 students were a key element on the barricades. On the whole, however, being educated was part of being a gentleman, and gentlemen were amateurs by definition, above the details of specialized knowledge, industry or trade, and radical politics. The university operated rather like a male finishing school, as a place where, it was hoped, one acquired moral stature, confidence and, most important, friends of an equal social standing. It was a far cry from the examination-punctuated atmosphere of university life today.

Science was very much the poor relation in the general advance in education in the 19th century. The Ecole Polytechnique in Paris (below) was, however, an influential exception. This prestigious institution was an incomparable breeding ground for great mathematicians and physicists, and was widely imitated abroad.

Mary Evans Picture Library

THE GREAT COMPOSERS

Robert Schumann

1810-1856

Robert Schumann, like his countryman Felix Mendelssohn, was a major figure of the early 19th-century Romantic movement in German art. Contemporaries considered him a very advanced composer, and he had great influence on succeeding artists as disparate as Brahms and Tchaikovsky. Despite his mental problems – he was always unbalanced and ended his days insane in a private lunatic asylum – Schumann's musical achievements were immense, most notably in the way he epitomized in his piano music the idioms of the Romantic movement: the apparent waywardness in the music's rhythm and the sudden changes of harmony. During his life-time, he was also justly famous for the insights of his music criticism for the Neue Zeitschrift für Musik. *He had the ability to recognize both the fully realized talents of his contemporary, Chopin, and in his last years, the promise of the young Brahms.*

In September 1853, when the young Johannes Brahms, with great trepidation, visited Robert Schumann, the distinguished composer and critic, he need not have worried. Schumann was overwhelmed, describing Brahms as a genius. The younger man was grateful to his 'revered master', and during Schumann's last terrible illness and after his death, helped the composer's wife, Clara. As the Composer's Life *describes, Clara Schumann, a pianist of great distinction in her own right, gave Schumann great happiness. The* Listener's Guide *analyzes Schumann's 'Spring' Symphony and Piano Concerto – both composed out of love for Clara – and describes Schumann's rôle in the development of music criticism, which was in part caused by the increased leisure time of the middle classes. In the Background describes how Schumann's contemporaries spent their time off, though much of the population was still occupied in the struggle for simple survival.*

COMPOSER'S LIFE

'Revered Master'

**Schumann – composer, critic and intellectual –
lived a turbulent yet at times brilliantly creative life.
A complex character, his decline was foreshadowed
in his increasingly erratic behaviour.**

Edimedia

Robert Schumann (above) was the essence of the Romantic composer. But though he railed against the conservatism of preceding generations, he was a generous and supportive critic of young composers.

Schumann was a prime-mover in the advancement of 19th century Romanticism; in his capacity as founder and editor of the famous German musical periodical *Neue Zeitschrift für Musik,* he was decisively influential in promoting the music of other young Romantic composers, among them Chopin and Brahms.

Strange as it may seem today, Schumann's music itself was less well-known in his day than were his activities as a writer. His music was the product of a nature so sensitive, and it spoke in so personal an idiom, that it was many years before it began to be accepted by the public.

Personality and appearance

As a young man, Schumann already showed two clear facets to his character. On the one hand he was extrovert, good company and energetic in his pursuit of new experiences, on the other, his avid passion for literature, especially Jean Paul Richter, E. T. A. Hoffman and the classics, encouraged the poetic side of his nature and turned him into a sensitive, retiring, thinker. A by-product of this second facet was a secretive trait, revealed in his penchant for pseudonyms and the so-called cyphers or coded messages he habitually hid in his music.

He also adopted two parallel pseudonyms for

Archiv für Kunst und Geschichte

As the precocious son of one of Zwickau's leading citizens, young Robert Schumann (left) starred easily at musical and literary gatherings in his hometown. He was largely self-taught, however, and did not receive formal musical training until he was 18.

himself: Florestan, the passionate hero, and Eusebius, the gentle introvert. These two 'characters' converse together in his diaries as early as 1831, when he was 21, and they soon enter into his music reviews. Later, they are named side-by-side as the actual composers of his music.

Sometimes he would display the most outrageous bad manners, especially if he had been subjected to what he considered to be bad music, or indeed any music badly performed. On these occasions he would speak his mind without restraint, or leave the company without a word. With hindsight, we may see in these general dual aspects of his nature the beginnings of the mental problems to which he was to fall victim in his last years.

Contemporary reports portray Schumann as a solidly-built man, upright but with a looseness about his stride almost as if his broad shoulders were boneless. He tended to narrow his blue eyes in an attempt to alleviate his short-sightedness, for which he habitually carried a *lorgnette* (a pair of glasses on a handle), and mischievous dimples appeared in his cheeks when he smiled. Long dark brown hair framed, and sometimes partly obscured, a face described as handsome in youth but ruddy and unhealthily chubby in his 40s. His dress was conservative and with time became more so: he usually wore black in later years.

Early years

Robert Alexander Schumann was born in Zwickau, Saxony, on June 8, 1810, the youngest of the five children of the bookseller, publisher and author August Schumann. His education, at first in a private school and later at Zwickau Lyceum, was supplemented by exposure to as much good literature in his father's bookshop as he could find the time to read, and by piano lessons from a local organist.

In 1826 Schumann experienced major grief with the deaths in quick succession of his only sister Emilie, whose suicide at the age of 19 released her from life as a total invalid; the composer Weber, with whom Schumann had planned to study composition; and of Schumann's father, who had succumbed at the age of 53 to a 'nervous disorder'. Some say that Schumann's later illness was inherited from his father.

However, Robert was soon to know happier times:

August Schumann (below right) died when Robert was 16, leaving his widow (below left) to steer her intense son into a safe career in law. But Robert's nervous temperament was alarmingly reminiscent of that of his father, and her efforts were in vain.

Hans Thoma's vision of the Rhineland (above). In 1829 Schumann enjoyed a dissolute holiday there, though he kept up his piano practice by pretending to be an interested customer in a piano shop.

Bildarchiv Preussischer Kulturbesitz

to Leipzig and his re-establishment as Wieck's pupil in Leipzig, whose house he shared for a while from October 1830. Wieck had written to Schumann's mother to the effect that if the young man were to study tenaciously for three years he would become a great pianist, but he frankly doubted Schumann's mental ability to sustain such a discipline. He suggested a six-month trial period and Schumann's mother agreed, thereby at last releasing him from all pretence at studying law. Wieck's attention, however, was not upon Robert Schumann. His daughter Clara, 11 years old, had become a brilliant pianist under her father's tuition and he now took her off on an extended concert tour.

Schumann filled the time by composing, writing, and inventing 'new and more suitable' names for his friends and acquaintances. Wieck became 'Meister Raro', the conductor Heinrich Dorn, who took over from Wieck as Schumann's music tutor, became 'The Music Director', and Clara Wieck became 'Zilia' (short for Cecilia, the patron saint of music). By July 1831 Schumann was calling himself 'Florestan and Eusebius'.

The independent composer

By the spring of 1832 Schumann had reached a turning-point. Lessons with Dorn and with Wieck had ceased, he had become financially independent on his 21st birthday due to his accession to a large part of his father's fortune, and he realized at last that his dream of becoming a great concert pianist would never become a reality. Amid circumstances that have never satisfactorily been explained, he had damaged one, or perhaps two, fingers on his right hand. He is known to have invented a sling device to strengthen the weak fourth finger and this has been blamed for permanently crippling his hand. Another theory, for which there is not much evidence, to account for the damage is that a treatment for syphilis had induced mercury poisoning

Hans Thoma 'Das Rhein bei Säckingen'/Bildarchiv Preussischer Kulturbesitz

young ladies started to become important to him. Happy he was, too, when drinking champagne, which he consumed in prodigious quantities from the age of 17 onwards.

Career

In 1828, Schumann was pushed into law school by his mother and his guardian. Once ensconced as a law student at Leipzig University, Robert made earnest endeavours to avoid every lecture. Instead, he spent his time at his desk concocting literary fantasies in Jean Paul Richter's manner, or at the keyboard practising and improvising. Exposure to Schubert's songs encouraged him to write a number of songs at this time. In August 1828, four months after his enrolment as a law student, Schumann began piano lessons with Friedrich Wieck in Leipzig.

Schumann's next act was to persuade his mother to allow him to transfer for a year to Heidelberg University. This was ostensibly to continue his law studies amid more stimulating surroundings and 'with the most famous professors'. But in reality it was so that he could be with an old friend, Gisbert Rosen. A bonus at Heidelberg was the presence of the 'famous professor' Anton Thibaut – who also just happened to be an enthusiastic musician! Schumann arrived in Heidelberg in May 1829 after a Rhineland holiday that left him penniless but happy.

Much of his year in Heidelberg was spent in socializing and living the unfettered life of an eligible young artist. Again, law studies were low in his priorities. His departure from Heidelberg led him back

Archiv für Kunst und Geschichte

J. P. F. Richter (left), better known by his pseudonym of Jean Paul, was Schumann's great literary hero. 'If everybody read Jean Paul,' wrote Schumann, 'we should be better but more unhappy.' Here Richter is shown at work in his garden, a suitable study for a great Romantic visionary.

From a very early age, Clara Wieck (right), was one of Europe's most outstanding pianists and her ambitious father's pride and joy. Friedrich Wieck's resistance to his brilliant daughter's betrothal to Schumann is understandable, because Clara became engaged just at the point in her career when her father was beginning to reap the financial rewards of his daughter's talent and his dedicated tuition. The form it took was, however, inexcusable.

morbidly in his grief. It was a self-centred grief that Schumann displayed, perhaps an attitude typical of one who could write in his diary the portentous line: 'I was obsessed by the thought that I might go mad.'

Schumann the journalist

Fortunately, a constructive influence entered his life at this time: the pianist Ludwig Schunke, a hearty and pleasant optimist, came to share Schumann's rooms, and in 1834 he was among the group, headed by Schumann and including Wieck, who launched the twice-weekly musical periodical *Neue Zeitschrift für Musik*. Most of the editorial chores fell to Schumann and he became happily immersed in the work. His group of friends were the living equivalent of the *Davidsbündler,* or 'Band of David', an imaginary brotherhood devised by the composer to fight Philistinism and the mediocre in music. The members were, naturally, Florestan, Eusebius and Meister Raro, together with any exalted musical spirit – Mozart's, Berlioz's – who happened by. The *Davidsbündler* fought out its battles in the pages of *Neue Zeitschrift für Musik*.

Much of Schumann's life revolved around the Wieck household, a centre for the 'real' *Davidsbündler* and a meeting place for composers visiting Leipzig, the attraction, of course, being the widely admired young pianist Clara. Schumann had become engaged in 1834 to Ernestine von Fricken, but a development in the Wieck house caused him to disentangle himself: Clara was growing up, and she and Schumann began to seek each other's company more and more.

The marketplace at Leipzig (below), a lively university town. Here, it was all too easy for an arch-romantic student such as Schumann to ignore lectures and 'drop out' into a congenial world of wine, women, song and endless passionate discourse on the arts.

that affected his extremities. Whatever the truth of the matter, his damaged hand precluded a concert career, and Schumann turned instead to composition, mainly for solo piano. He also attempted, and nearly completed, a symphony, the first movement of which was played on 18 November 1832, in Zwickau, and again, in greatly revised form, at Clara Wieck's *Grand Concerts* on 29 April 1833, in Leipzig.

Severe depression set in during 1833. That summer he suffered from persistent fever, and in October his brother Karl's wife, 25 year-old Rosalie, died, and his brother Julius died in November. In letters to his mother he appears to take pleasure in wallowing

The Wieck family war

Alarmed at what he considered an ill-advised, if not unhealthy, match between the wayward Schumann and his 16-year-old daughter, old Wieck resisted with every weapon at his disposal. A letter forbidding Schumann to call at his house was the first shot, and he informed his daughter that there would be real shots if the composer disobeyed. Clara herself was confined to the house and told that all the money she had earned during her concert tours was held in trust until her 21st birthday, and not one penny would be hers if she married before then without his consent.

For her part, Clara was profoundly distressed, for she reciprocated the love Schumann so ardently expressed. The couple managed to exchange notes and even the surreptitious kiss at rare, secret meetings. For Robert, this was not enough. In desperation, he wrote to Wieck imploring him to relent and make two young people happy. At the subsequent meeting, the old man so confounded Schumann by parading a host of conflicting arguments, malicious insults, doubtful concessions and accusations before him, that the composer retired in almost suicidal depression.

At length the whole sad business was referred to the courts. The slow-moving legal wheels were further retarded by Wieck's refusal to attend hearings. Meanwhile, he did his best to ruin the considerable reputation Clara had built for herself by writing malicious, and often falsely-signed, letters to everyone he could think of. It is difficult to believe that any father could bear such vicious malice towards a

The Schumanns seven years into an idyllic marriage that took place after a nerve-racking courtship. There were strains on the union, however, due to the competing requirements of their separate careers – she could not practise while he composed, and his pride was wounded by her greater fame as a pianist.

Compared with Leipzig, Dresden (below), where the Schumanns moved in 1844, was a stuffy and conservative place, but initially it had a calming effect on Schumann's already precarious mental state.

daughter as Wieck did to Clara.

The court duly heard Wieck's objections and on 4 January, 1840, a decision was made. All of Wieck's objections were overruled save one: that concerning Schumann's excessive drinking. This charge Wieck was required to prove, but since he failed to do so within a specified time, the final decision in favour of Schumann and Clara was made in August 1840, four years after Wieck's declaration of war. By a stroke of ironic timing, the wedding took place at Schönefeld, near Leipzig, on 12 September 1840; the very next day, her 21st birthday, Clara would have been legally free to marry whomsoever she pleased!

Creativity

Schumann's composing energy had been severely sapped by the long battle, but in 1840 he turned from writing for solo piano to produce a whole host of songs, among them his famous *Liederkreis, Frauenliebe und -leben, Dichterliebe,* and many more. When this mine of songs became temporarily exhausted, Schumann turned to the orchestra. His 'Spring' Symphony was written in the depths of winter (23 January to 20 February 1841) and performed in March, and in May he completed his *Fantasie* in A minor for piano and orchestra which was later to become the first movement of his Piano Concerto. Two other substantial orchestral works were to appear before the end of the year, but his restless creativity, stimulated by the sublime happiness of his new life with Clara, was pushing him into new spheres: 1842 was to see his two greatest chamber works, the Piano Quintet and the Piano Quartet.

On the road with Clara

Meanwhile, Clara followed her own career. This inevitably led to conflicting engagements; in March 1842 the couple were parted, Schumann in Leipzig,

Even dull Dresden did not escape the revolutionary fervour of 1848–49. But when the barricades went up, Schumann, unlike Wagner, did not man them. During the fighting he took refuge with his family outside Dresden.

completed in June. The year also saw a reconciliation between Clara and her father and an uneasy truce between the old man and Robert. The first half of 1844 was taken up with a successful concert tour of Russia by the couple. However, it was only successful as far as Clara was concerned, since her fame had preceded her, but Schumann, despite directing his own 'Spring' Symphony in St Petersburg and attending a performance of his Quintet in Moscow, with Clara playing the piano part, was conscious of taking a second place to his wife's concert achievements.

Upon their return to Leipzig Schumann relinquished editorship of *Neue Zeitschrift* in order to concentrate upon a new passion: opera. All that issued from his tired brain were some pieces based on Goethe's *Faust,* and even this effort, meagre in comparison with the years 1840–42, cost him dearly in mental stamina. The strain of the Russian tour, with its attendant professional frustration, and a general feeling of depression, abruptly crystallized into a total nervous breakdown. Even music, he reported, 'cuts into my nerves like knives'. For a week he was unable to sleep and could barely walk; doctors were powerless to help except to recommend a complete change of scene. Consequently, the family moved to Dresden in December 1844 and slowly Schumann's health began to improve.

During 1845 he completed the Piano Concerto and began work on another symphony, but the latter took almost a year to complete, and it was during this time that new menaces assailed him: vertigo, and a deterioration of his hearing – further signs of the

Clara in Copenhagen, while Wieck gleefully put about the rumour that the marriage had collapsed. Alone, Schumann gazed into beermugs and studied counterpoint, sometimes simultaneously. Clara's career, however, was to be punctuated by pregnancies. The first child, a daughter, had arrived on 1 September 1841, and seven more children were to follow up to June 1854.

It was the turn of choral music in 1843, but only one work emerged: *Das Paradies und die Peri,* an oratorio,

Before moving to Düsseldorf (right), Schumann had been perturbed to learn that the town boasted a lunatic asylum, for he disliked hearing anything that reminded him of insanity. His misgivings proved sadly justified because his mental condition deteriorated seriously in Düsseldorf.

This posthumous portrait of Robert Schumann (1859), though probably idealized, still conveys the despair of a man gripped by acute nervous crises beyond the competence of contemporary medicine.

Archiv für Kunst und Geschichte

After a final breakdown in 1854, Robert Schumann was committed to Dr Richarz's private asylum at Endenich near Bonn (below), where he died in 1856.

Photo Harlingue-Viollet

progressive collapse of his nervous system. A two-month holiday at Norderney, a North Sea island, brought temporary respite, and in November 1846 the couple set off on tour for Vienna in a new mood of optimism. It was misplaced.

The audiences there applauded Schumann's music dutifully, but seemed to have forgotten how welcome they had made Clara some years before. She was still a wonder, but no longer a wonder child. In Prague, however, where the couple gave two concerts on their journey home, they were enthusiastically received, and a subsequent trip to Berlin also encouraged them. Further operatic endeavours occupied Schumann during 1847 and 1848 (*Genoveva,* more work on *Faust,* and the overture *Manfred*), and he entered the most productive period of his life.

Late inspiration

From this time, music literally poured out of him for some six years. Even the revolutionary unrest of May 1849 failed to stem the flow completely, but it did force the family to flee Dresden for two months after a last-minute escape through a back door to avoid Schumann's conscription into a hastily set-up militia.

Clara continued giving concerts and Robert's music was gaining recognition, but attempts to consolidate his position in Dresden were unsuccessful, as was his application for the post of music director at Leipzig. However, in September 1850 the family moved to Düsseldorf; Schumann had accepted the post there of municipal music director. After a period of adjustment, and despite further mental and physical debility early in 1852, his composing urge returned. He also had quarrels with the authorities over his running of the city's musical activities. Schumann was temperamentally unsuited to maintain the training and discipline of his musicians, a fact betrayed by a serious lowering in artistic standards.

The end

The trouble in Düsseldorf and a number of working visits to other musical centres during 1853 finally destroyed nerves made frail by prolonged overwork. In February 1854, hallucinations and 'very strong, painful aural symptoms' occurred and his nights were filled with heavenly and hellish dreams. Convinced that his fears of insanity were at last vindicated, he threw himself into the Rhine, but was rescued and brought home in a fearful state of mental derangement. Doctors forbade Clara to see him, and on 4 March 1854 he was taken to a private asylum at Endenich, near Bonn. Clara did not see him until more than two years later, by which time he was unable to utter intelligible words.

During those two final years he experienced periods of relative stability and corresponded with Clara and with several friends. He even accepted visitors, Brahms among them. Schumann's mind was still spasmodically active: he continued to compose, though nothing important emerged, and towards the end Brahms disturbed him obsessively making alphabetical lists of towns and countries.

On 29 July, 1856, at 4pm, he died in his cell. His span of 46 years was over.

Schumann's music did not break barriers, neither was he ahead of his time. On the contrary, it tended to ignore the formal confines of the classical period in the interest of self-expression, and it was emphatically of its time in that it wholeheartedly adopted the Romantic fervour generated by authors, poets and painters early in the 19th century.

LISTENER'S GUIDE

Orchestral works

Schumann's 'Spring' Symphony and his Piano Concerto, composed during the idyllic early months of marriage, were inspired by his love for his wife Clara.

Symphony no. 1 in B flat major, op. 38 ('Spring')

Both the 'Spring' Symphony and the Piano Concerto no. 1 had their origins in 1841. Robert Schumann had married Clara Wieck, the famous concert pianist, the previous year, and it was as a result of her encouragement that he turned from the intimate worlds of song and piano music that had occupied most of his composing activity up to that time, to the 'public' utterances of symphony and concerto. Clara had long felt that the breadth of Schumann's imagination required the wider dimensions offered by the orchestra; but it is unlikely that Schumann needed a great deal of persuasion since the composition of both Symphony and Concerto had been on his mind for a number of years.

Although the 'Spring' Symphony is entitled Symphony no. 1, Schumann had in fact completed three movements and sketched in a fourth for a symphony in G minor between 1832–3. He had also sketched in four movements for a symphony in C minor between 1840–1, which he later used in other works. However, the 'Spring' Symphony, his first finished symphony, was tackled with a far greater feeling of urgency. The whole was sketched out in four days from 23 to 26 January 1841. The orchestration took from 27 January to 20 February.

First performance
It was first performed under Mendelssohn's direction on 31 March at the Leipzig Gewandhaus, at a concert given by Clara Schumann. After the première in Leipzig, which also marked Clara's return to the concert platform after her marriage, the Symphony was performed in Bremen and Hamburg in 1842, again at concerts at which Clara appeared. But poor Schumann's entry into the symphonic arena failed to meet with the enthusiasm and appreciation he had expected, for subsequent invitations to musical centres tended to be for Clara alone. But if the 'Spring' Symphony met with a cool response at the time, today it stands as one of the best-loved of all Romantic symphonies, its so-called 'faults' of pianistic writing and thick, scoring easily outweighed by its charm and ardour.

A lithograph of Schumann in 1839, two years before he composed the 'Spring' Symphony and the Piano Concerto in A minor.

Archiv für Kunst und Geschichte

Programme notes
Schumann was probably most encouraged to begin the 'Spring' Symphony by his examination – and the subsequent first performance by Mendelssohn at a Leipzig Gewandhaus concert in 1840 – of Franz Schubert's Symphony no. 9 in C, ('The Great'), which Schumann called 'The Symphony of Heavenly Length'. But it was probably the idea of writing a symphony, rather than Schubert's work, that influenced him, since the two symphonies, Schubert's last and Schumann's first, inhabit totally different worlds.

Schumann's inspiration for composition came from within, from a desire to widen his creative experience and explore different forms. He was aware that he had temporarily exhausted the rich veins of piano music and song, and was so encouraged by Clara's faith that he was ready to expand his expressive language. We may even share with Schumann his transition from the smaller to the larger form, for in the Symphony we find distinct traces of both song and piano textures and signs of Schumann's developing confidence in writing for a full orchestra.

First movement: Andante un poco maestoso – Allegro molto vivace
The opening notes are based upon the rhythm of a line from a spring poem by Adolph Böttger:

This phrase is immediately repeated as all the woodwind and strings join the brass in joyful acclamation. The rest of the slow introduction consists of a series of descents and ascents by lower strings,

sharp chords on brass, woodwind and drums, an undulating murmur that starts on cellos and works its way upward through violas and violins. Behind it all, there are frequent references to that opening brass fanfare. Gradually the music accelerates, screwing the tension tighter, until it is released by an outburst on four horns, and the main part of the movement arrives.

The *Allegro molto vivace* (fast with much exuberance) starts with that very same fanfare, but almost four times as fast. It takes off like a March hare, horns in hot pursuit with the fanfare rhythm, but the horns are the first to tire. This brings a moment of repose: a tentative tune with clarinets and bassoons emerges, gradually gaining assurance with flutes and oboes. The music then urges forward once more to an emphatic conclusion.

The development section now begins with that ubiquitous fanfare rhythm, passed freely from strings to wind and back again, until a new theme on oboes and clarinets appears, only to be swallowed up amid the general excitement. The fanfare returns, accompanied by a new voice: the triangle, an instrument used but rarely in symphonies adds brilliance as a solo flute plays the continuation.

Soon the new theme reappears, this time

Botticelli's famous painting of the Primavera, *like the first movement of Schumann's Symphony, is a celebration of the Awakening of Spring.*

Sandro Botticelli. 'La Primavera'. Uffizi, Florence/Scala

giving way to a gradual increase in excitement; clearly something important is about to happen. It is the opening fanfare, back to its original stately tempo but now shouted out by full orchestra – the recapitulation has arrived and the movement retraces its steps. A long crescendo leads, not to the final chords as expected, but to a surprise: for a moment the strings recall Schumann's gently romantic piano music, before the solo flute (with a rising phrase surely borrowed from Beethoven's 'Pastoral' Symphony) heralds the final flourish.

Second movement: Larghetto

Nearly a song without words, the Larghetto is a placid picture of a spring evening of romance. Most noteworthy is the graceful theme played by cellos, later extended to horns and woodwind. As it sinks to rest, Schumann surprises us again: three trombones darken the mood with a solemn statement, and the music awaits development.

Third movement: Scherzo – Molto vivace

With hardly a pause, the Scherzo bursts in taking up the trombones' statement from the end of the previous movement in determined mood. Soon, however, the 'surprise' moment of romance, from near the end of the first movement, enters playfully on woodwind, with strings swirling and dancing an accompaniment, before earnestness returns.

Most scherzo movements have a central contrasting section (the *Trio*) which, in Beethoven's case, often returns to make a double sandwich of the movement. In the

This painting by Sir John Lavery of a woman and girl in an orchard conveys the dreamy, tranquil mood of the more reflective passages in the 'Spring' Symphony.

Schumann originally entitled the slow second movement of his Symphony no. 1 'Evening' and this picture of Springtime by Alfred East has the same calm peaceful quality.

Fourth movement: Allegro animato e grazioso
A brilliant, syncopated flourish – then a giggling, frolicking scrap of a tune like a Gilbert and Sullivan patter song that disintegrates comically amid sharp punctuation:

A new idea, borrowed from Schumann's own piano piece *Kreisleriana,* trots in on oboes and bassoons, and is immediately brought to order by the rising flourish on strings. This is soon transformed and extended into a grand paragraph that gives way to the development.

The development section takes its cue from the opening flourish and seems to prepare for a solemn climax, but Schumann surprises us yet again. After the music slows to a halt, horns awaken the flute into a delicate cadenza that can lead only to the 'patter song', and the movement restates its ideas. A tightening of the rhythm and a tying of loose ends, and this joyful, ardent Symphony rushes to a close.

'Spring' Symphony, Schumann reaches back as far as the 18th century *divertimento* form and interpolates two entirely different trio sections. The first trio alternates a simple rhythmic figure between strings and wind; it seems to suggest the first movement's fanfare, although this never quite crystallizes. The second trio is a chattering creation, swelling and subsiding several times before giving way to a brief final recollection of the Scherzo. The movement closes quietly with fragments of the first trio. This movement could almost be described as the month of March in sound: in like a lion; out like a lamb.

'Merry playmates' was the name Schumann gave to the lively third movement, and Peter Breughel's Dancing Peasants *gives some idea of the zest and energy of the music.*

Piano Concerto in A minor, op. 54

This is Schumann's only completed piano concerto, though not his first attempt at such a work. In 1829 he was working on a Concerto in F minor which remained unfinished. Between 1829 and 1831 he composed a Concerto in F which was also never finished and in early 1839 he wrote the first movement for a Concerto in D minor.

Alongside the Tchaikovsky First and Grieg's only completed piano concerto Schumann's is amongst the best-loved of all Romantic Piano Concertos. In many ways it is a gentler, more sensitive work than its rivals, yet it lacks nothing in bravura display. It was written by a pianist for a pianist and displays a unique understanding of the instrument. Schumann, despite his injured hand, always composed at the piano until 1845, and Clara Schumann often performed the work during her many concert tours.

Schumann completed the first movement in Leipzig in May 1841 as *Fantasie* in A minor for Piano and Orchestra; he did not return to finish the rest of the Concerto until 1845 in Dresden. Clara gave the first performance in December of that year in Dresden with Ferdinand Hiller conducting. She also gave its second performance on 1 January 1846, when Mendelssohn, who is said to have disliked the work, conducted it at a Leipzig *Gewandhaus* concert where it was highly esteemed.

Programme notes

While the 'Spring' Symphony has strong literary associations, the Piano Concerto has no *programme* (guidelines) whatever to help us understand its 'meaning'. Quite simply, it is a Romantic study in absolute music, although one may be forgiven for reading into it an expression of the love Schumann felt for Clara. *Affettuoso*, in the first movement, after all, means 'affectionately'.

First movement: Allegro affettuoso

Schumann had a great deal of musical material to present so he wasted no time. With the minimum of preparation – a single orchestral unison – he begins to unfold his ideas, which occur in great profusion.

That opening unison brings a striking statement which tumbles down the keyboard. It gives way immediately to a downward-curving oboe melody, richly harmonized, and extended by the soloist:

Example 1

This is followed by a serious motif upon which the piano and orchestra agree. In turn, this gives way to an idea in shorter notes on strings, which the piano is reluctant at first to adopt, but it grows in confidence and is taken up by the full orchestra. A bold piano theme then develops into a restatement of the earlier

Schumann was inspired to write the Piano Concerto by his wife Clara – a brilliant concert pianist. The lithograph shows the composer listening to her playing.

The Mansell Collection

This Girl on a Swing by Lancret has the graceful charm and ease of the Piano Concerto. The music and the painting share a feeling of youthful gaiety.

oboe melody, passionately presented by the soloist and extended in a clarinet-led episode, amidst which occurs yet another idea, a playful tune first on oboe, then on piano. A further piano phrase, rising and falling, makes way for a climax.

A change to a slower tempo and a new rhythm (Andante espressivo) ushers in the development, much of which is taken up by a meditative discussion between piano and clarinet. Then all previous ideas are recapitulated in the same order but with slight changes and a more urgent treatment of the opening melody. But instead of building up at the end to an orchestral climax, it now brings a long cadenza for the piano solo, and the movement closes with a march-like passage, led by oboe.

Second movement: Intermezzo – Andantino grazioso

A more delicate movement could hardly be imagined. It comes as a perfect contrast to the first movement and forms a suitable introduction to the ebullient finale, to which it is connected. The first part of the slow movement itself divides into three: a light melody announced by piano, a more earnest woodwind theme, and then a return to the light melody. A graceful cello theme

with a delicate piano decoration occupies the central position and is subjected to gentle examination and modification before the three-part first section returns. This unexpectedly leads to a two-fold recollection of the opening oboe theme from the first movement.

Third movement: Allegro vivace

Abruptly launched in headstrong mood, the main theme of the finale is a radically transformed version of that opening oboe theme. It dominates the movement, but it courteously makes way for a second subject in cross-rhythm (two beats against three), a leaping piano figure related to the piano phrase at the end of the first movement, and a march which attracts the orchestral strings more readily than the piano, which embellishes it with rapid notes. The development section reminds us that Schumann had made an intensive study of counterpoint during the early months of 1845, for it toys with fugal technique.

When all this material has been restated, Schumann builds an exciting coda upon the march's rippling piano accompaniment. The end of the Concerto is vigorous, joyful and confident.

Great interpreters

Decca International/Lichfield

Sir George Solti (conductor)

Solti, though adopting British nationality in 1972, was originally Hungarian, being born in Budapest in 1912. His musical talent was recognized early on, and he trained as a pianist at the Liszt academy in Budapest under Szekely, Kodály, Bartok and Dohnanyi. It was as a pianist that he started his professional career with the Budapest Opera. After working with Toscanini at the 1936 and 1937 Salzburg Festivals, he made his conducting debut in Budapest in 1938 with *Figaro*.

Due to his Jewish descent, Solti was

The conductor, Sir Georg Solti (above).
The pianist, Radu Lupu (below).

finally compelled to quit an increasingly fascist Hungary, and he spent the War years in Switzerland as a concert pianist. In the immediate post-War period he became established in Munich as the musical director of the Bayerische Staatoper, continuing in this post until 1952. This period saw the beginning of both his and Munich's high postwar reputation for operatic excellence.

1952, the year of his move to Frankfurt, also saw him making his debut at the Edinburgh Festival, while he made his first trip to the U.S. the following year. The rest of that decade saw him emerge as one of the great modern conductors, both live and on record; a man of iron will and determination to have the music played the way he saw it. An admirer of both Toscanini and Fürtwangler, he strove to combine the often opposed conducting philosophies of these two giants, and by 1959, and his debut at Covent Garden, his operatic reputation was secure. His ten years as director at the Royal Opera, 1961–'71 saw him complete not only the first commercially-released Ring Cycle, but a highly-praised cycle of Mahler Symphonies as well as numerous other operas, from Strauss to Mozart. Since then he has become a well-known musical personality and was awarded a K.B.E. in 1971.

Solti's style is bold, decisive and often up-tempo: both his Mozart and Wagner have been hailed as either brilliant or shallow, depending on the critical viewpoint.

Radu Lupu (pianist)

Lupu emerged in the 1970s as one of the leading pianists of the immediate postwar

generation. Born in November 1945 in Romania, Lupu commenced piano lessons when he was six years old, and in 1957, at the age of 12, he made his public debut in his native country. During this period of his life he was studying with Muzicescu, a teacher of the legendary pianist Dinu Lipatti, before winning in 1963 a scholarship to the Moscow Conservatory. He remained a student there until 1969, while at the same time competing in, and winning, two international piano competitions, the Van Cliburn in 1966, and the Enescu International in 1967. In the same year as he completed his studies, 1969, he won the prestigious Leeds Piano Competition and proceeded on to his first London recital, which was greeted by great critical acclaim.

Since then, Lupu has steadily increased his international reputation, making frequent tours in both Europe and America. This concert career was paralleled by a long series of recordings in solo, chamber and orchestral settings which clearly outlined his main areas of musical interest. A proven interpreter of Schubert, Schumann and Brahms piano music, he also scored a significant success in his recording, with the renowned violinist Szymon Goldberg, of the complete Mozart Sonatas for Violin and Piano. Other records include the complete Beethoven Piano Concertos and works by Debussy and Franck.

Decca International

FURTHER LISTENING

Symphony no. 3 in E flat major op. 97 ('Rhenish')
Nine years after composing the 'Spring' Symphony, Robert Schumann arrived with Clara, in the Rhenish city of Düsseldorf. The Third Symphony, written in five movements, depicts in musical terms the life and landscape of the Rhineland – in particular its most famous building, Cologne Cathedral. Of Schumann's four symphonies, this is by far the most programmatic.

Cello Concerto in A minor, op. 129
This Concerto, dating from the same period as the 'Rhenish' symphony, was written in the incredibly short span of 15 days. It shows Schumann at his most intimate. 'I cannot write a concerto for the virtuosos', he declared earlier in his career and indeed this work offers little scope for conventional virtuosity. It is nevertheless full of endearing music which is remarkable for its freshness and spontaneity; and the linking of its three movements into a continuous whole reflects the Romantic movement's search for unity.

Overture in E flat minor, op. 115 ('Manfred')
Outstanding among Schumann's orchestral works, this character study of Byron's hero is a sombre musical masterpiece.

Understanding music: musical criticism

In his day, Schumann was perhaps as well known as a critic as a composer – and his articles in the *Neue Zeitschrift für Musik* reached a far wider audience than much of his music ever did. With the growth of the middle class audience in the early 19th century, the critic assumed a more and more important role in the dissemination and appreciation of music. In the absence of broadcasts and recording, musical journals were often the only way of keeping abreast of developments, and middle class music lovers devoured criticism keenly.

At this time journals multiplied rapidly – the first of these, the *Allgemeine musikalische Zeitung,* was founded in Leipzig. In such periodicals, the works of Mozart, Beethoven and Schubert were first criticised – and were generally more favourably received than many of the more sentimental biographers would have us believe. The well-known critic E. T. A. Hoffmann acclaimed as early as 1809 that Beethoven was among the spiritual leaders of mankind.

It was only a question of time before composers themselves entered the literary arena, a course which would have been unthinkable for such earlier composers as Haydn or Mozart. In 1834, Schlesinger founded the *Gazette musicale de Paris* expressly for this purpose and in the same year, Schumann founded his *Neue Zeitschrift für Musik.*

By now there were some half dozen musical journals with reviews of new music, general articles, short stories, poems and original musical compositions.

Like Weber before him, Schumann had contributed to the *Allgemeine musikalische Zeitung* and had a high regard for its founder, Friedrich Rochlitz. Under Rochlitz's successor, Gottfried Wilhelm Fink, however, standards deteriorated badly. What appalled Schumann about the *Allgemeine* under Fink was its oppressive conservatism and, its lack of interest in anything but homegrown music and, above all, its apparent inability to distinguish between good music and bad. Schumann was determined that in his new publication, all this would be put right.

The first edition of *Neue Zeitschrift für Musik* saw Schumann hailing Chopin as a genius, and throughout the ten years that he wrote for the journal, he pursued a policy of encouraging young composers, including, in his last article, the 20 year-old Brahms. But he also strongly believed in putting contemporary music in a historical perspective, acclaiming the works of Beethoven, Schubert, Berlioz and Weber on the one hand, while also directing his readers' attention to earlier composers like Bach, Handel, Scarlatti, Couperin and Glück.

Perhaps in his championing of New Music he was at times over-zealous – many of his protégés sunk into obscurity – but in general he exercised a progressive influence. As he himself stated, 'the critic who dares not to attack what is bad is but a half-hearted supporter of what is good'.

By the middle of the century there was a reaction to the more extravagant side of musical criticism. The leading figure in this reaction was Eduard Hanslick who dominated the Viennese musical press for 50 years from 1855–1904. Today, Hanslick is remembered chiefly as an enemy of Wagner (who somewhat unkindly pilloried him as the character Beckmesser in his opera *Die Meistersinger*). He felt it necessary to reassert the claims of music as sound rather than propaganda as he saw the writings of Wagner. He viewed Wagner's new innovations as an end rather than a beginning and for Wagner alone; 'Whoever follows will break his neck.' Viewed with 20th century hindsight who would dispute this claim?

Print compositors making up blocks of type (left). With the availability of cheap printing facilities and a growing circle of music enthusiasts in the middle class, musical journals proliferated in the early 19th century. Schumann's crusading journal, the Neue Zeitschrift für Musik, *was just one – though perhaps the most important – of many.*

IN THE BACKGROUND

Freude! Freude!

Schumann's Germany witnessed the rise of a new middle-class phenomenon – leisure time. And although, for many, survival itself was the main consideration, the wealthy continued to entertain on a lavish scale.

Leisure has become something we now take for granted: time to spend with our family, time to read, time to write letters, time to relax and pursue hobbies. Yet leisure is very much a modern invention – a late by-product of the industrial revolution. If we read between the lines of letters and diaries in early 19th-century Germany, we can see many modern leisure activities in a primitive form, as well as the remains of earlier social systems going back to the middle ages.

Germany in 1800 was much closer to the middle ages than France or Britain. While England advanced into industrialization, the political convulsions in Paris set a pattern that influenced the rest of the world. Germany did not exist as a country. It was a patchwork of states connected by dreadful roads. After the Napoleonic Wars, the German Confederation was set up with 39 separate principalities, but even within the state of Prussia, the largest state, there were numerous customs zones: a traveller going from Hamburg to

Berlin had to pass through 63 frontier posts. And the roads were so bad that to travel, in 1815, from Brunswick to Lübeck, about 130 miles, took three days.

Communications were almost non-existent across large areas of the countryside. Over 90 per cent of the population lived in farms and small villages. The great majority of people lived and died without ever seeing a town, let alone attending a theatrical performance or buying a magazine. Villagers would refer to a place three miles away as 'abroad'. Ironically, one result of these primitive conditions was a high degree of hospitality. Travellers in early 19th-century Germany were made welcome and pumped for news of the outside world simply because people felt so cut off.

Peasant life

One of the key leisure activities in these isolated rural communities was centred around the spinning room.

In fine weather the beer garden (left) was a popular family attraction, providing an opportunity to eat and drink, show off one's best outfit and hear the local musicians.

By today's standards, life in Germany during the first half of the last century was serene and uncomplicated – at least, for those above the poverty line. The timeless and classless pleasure of lakeside fishing was a pastime enjoyed by many.

During the long winter months, when there was no agricultural work to be done, the villagers – men and women, married and unmarried – would gather in the larger rooms to spin together, and to sing and gossip as they spun. This social habit continued to be popular after hand spinning was no longer a vital activity.

If any traveller passed through the village, he was encouraged to visit the spinning room and tell of his travels. If he had any books or newspapers, he was encouraged to read them aloud. The spinning room became an important social centre around the time of the Reformation, and the custom persisted until well into the 19th century.

In fact, as young people began to leave the land and head for the city and as village society disintegrated, the spinning room became a last bastion of the old way of life. They sang of how much better off they were in the countryside, the songs becoming more idyllic and sentimental.

The spinning room was attacked both by the clergy and the police – because there the peasants socialized without anyone in authority over them. The Church denounced the spinning rooms as dens of iniquity because young, unmarried men and women would drink together, sing songs together, and perhaps even worse ... Certainly the spinning room functioned as an unofficial marriage market and as a centre for allowing romance to blossom.

It was a spinning room that provided the starting point for Wagner's opera *The Flying Dutchman*: it is there that Senta and her maidens sing of the haunted ship and its ghostly crew. In the spinning room Senta conceived the idea of saving the soul of the Flying Dutchman.

Other accounts of peasant life in the early 19th century suggest scenes from the middle ages. As one

The hub of rural community social life for gossip, news, romance and conversation was the spinning room (above left). But to the police and the clergy it represented a potential hot-bed of agitation and moral degeneracy. The authorities considered there was little to fear, however, from the musical soirées favoured by the middle class (above).

The coffee house (left) was the middle-class equivalent of the spinning room – except that it was strictly a male preserve. The coffee drinkers caught up on the news and exchanged views on the constantly changing political scene.

Westphalian peasant of the time remembered it:

'Two or three times a year the peasants had permission to play games in the main hall of the farm. They played blind man's buff and games like that. They were jumping and singing and falling all over the place, shouting and laughing. Until at the appointed hour, the head man appeared, like the figure of Fate himself, and ordered them all to go to bed.'

The leisure time of the lower classes was supervised as much as possible. One book of advice to the lady of the house suggested:

'Servant girls are not supposed to go to dances if their morality is threatened, but you must tell them that when you hire them. It is better to compensate them with money or with innocent pleasures. You must never forget that you have a duty to supervise the morals of the servants. It is incomprehensible why some ladies give little knick-knacks to their maids, and thus encourage their vanity, and so the maid can be led into sin.'

The middle class
For the lady of the house, leisure was increasing as the extended family shrank during the 19th century. Around 1800 it was common for a rural household to contain several generations, as well as the servants and the apprentices that worked with the master. During the 19th century this was gradually whittled down to the nuclear family we are used to: parents and children. These shrinking households gave the lady of the house more time for her own amusement, and more time to spend with the children. Among this new middle-class, and mainly female, audience there was a

craze for reading popular novels.

Goethe's *The Sorrows of Young Werther* made him famous overnight in 1774 with the tragedy of a young hero who is not only disappointed in love, but also feels alienated from the world around him. With its intense emotional aura, and its vivid account of the growth and despair of love, *Young Werther* established a new uniform for sensitive young men of means all over Europe: a blue coat worn over yellow breeches. Napoleon was reported to have read the novel at least seven times; and several young men actually committed suicide in careful imitation of the book's doomed hero. The novels of Jean Paul Richter also achieved a huge popularity, and his lush romantic style strongly influenced the prose of Robert Schumann.

There was no shortage of critics who complained that young women were ruining their minds by reading too many frivolous novels. A more uplifting type of book began to appear at this time: detailed accounts of household management to tell young wives how to set up and run their establishments. From these books it becomes clear how many activities that are now part of shopping and a consumer society used to take place inside the middle-class home. Hair dressing, making soap and candles, brewing beer, cultivating indoor plants, and the massive task of stocking the larder for the winter months with pickles and preserves are all explained within these manuals.

The attitude towards children in these works is quite sensitive and imaginative – a long way from the clichés of a strict 'Germanic' upbringing that might be expected. In the early 19th century several children's classics were published based on older sources – the Brothers Grimms' fairy stories from German folklore, and the more grotesque stories of *Struwwelpeter* by Heinrich Hoffmann. The fact that these books are still

Street entertainers like the organ grinder (left) brought popular melodies to the very front doors of urban dwellers. In the same vein travelling fairs with booths and sideshows provided a cheap form of entertainment for the populace.

In this painting by Spitzweg a German family is gently satirized taking a Sunday stroll. But walking was a serious matter: for many it was not only a free and readily available pleasure, but also their only means of getting about.

popular with children today suggests that the emphasis on domestic happiness was not totally without foundation.

After 1848 the passion for reading romantic fiction began to diminish and the reading craze moved towards a new type of magazine. Technical improvements in printing made magazines cheaper and enormous print runs possible. One massive but typical success was called *Gartenlaube* ('Garden Bower') and first appeared in 1853. At the end of the first year it had attracted 5000 readers. Twenty years later it had a circulation of 380,000 with its combination of romantic fiction and domestic advice. Improvements in printing and distribution had created a new market for a new type of magazine – the forerunners of the women's magazines which today sell in their millions.

The theatre

A country consisting of few towns, bad roads, and little cultural unity will not quickly give rise to a thriving theatre. Over a period of 70 years, from the appearance in the 1770s of Germany's first dramatist of world stature, Gotthold Ephraim Lessing, the German theatre struggled heroically on to the stage. By the year 1840 there were reckoned to be 65 theatres in German-speaking countries, employing about 5000 actors, musicians and singers.

This theatre was created out of several earlier traditions but chiefly from the touring German theatre companies which had been thriving since about 1700.

For the well-heeled, artistes from Italy were bringing opera to the courts and also occasional works of mime deriving from the *comedia dell 'arte* tradition – the popular improvised comedies of 18th-century Italy. These highly trained troupes often brought sophisticated stage effects with them, so that cities could appear to be consumed by fire, and chariots could ascend into the sky.

Bildarchiv Preussischer Kulturbesitz

The association between students and hell-raising is not confined to this century. Duelling, though officially outlawed, was widely practised among students as a demonstration of personal valour and defiance against the establishment.

as the master of dramatic form, an influence discernible in the historical works of Goethe and Schiller which were staged at Weimar.

Goethe worked hard to improve the social standing of actors and to improve their discipline as a troupe: performers were fined if they missed their cues; one actress who absented herself for a week was punished on her return by being confined to quarters under military guard.

A visitor to the Weimar theatre noticed that the middle class and students sat downstairs, the courtiers and officials in the balcony, and the masses in the top gallery. The students could be particularly trouble-some in the summer, especially during the cherry season: they would eat fruit in the stalls and bombard the actors with cherry-stones. Although Goethe invited the actors to his home and attempted to improve their social standing, he did not find this easy. A contract for one troublesome married couple laid down that they should separate if Herr Burgdorf continued to create scandals by assaulting his wife in public!

It was a disagreement with a difficult actress which finally led Goethe to resign from the theatre. While he was temporarily absent in April 1817, Karoline Jagemann (who had become the mistress of Weimar's ruler, Karl August) staged a production of the play *Aubrey de Mont Didier's Dog* which featured a performing poodle in the lead role. Since Goethe had worked so hard to increase the cultural prestige of theatre, and raise the social status of actors above that of circus animals, he was deeply upset and left the direction of the theatre to Fräulein Jagemann.

A third strand was provided by academics and writers who were looking for a way of forging a distinctly German drama by the mid 18th century. By 1800, several German towns had companies which they would call a 'National Theatre' to distinguish them from travelling players, and from the foreign companies maintained by the courts.

Goethe's role
Of great importance in creating a German Theatre was the work done by Goethe at the court of Weimar, where he directed a company of professional players from 1791 to 1817. Here the emphasis moved away from French convention towards emulating Shakespeare

Mid 19th century theatre
By 1840 the leading actor-managers of Germany, such as Iffland in Berlin, lived in sumptuous villas and were as celebrated as Garrick in London. The dominant form of drama was historical and heroic, under the

Dramatists and critics and all those who wanted to see the German theatre grow in stature may have taken the art form with great seriousness, but for the theatre goers themselves it was a chance to be as boisterous as they liked.

Guerard 'Bal de l'Opéra'. Carnavalet/Bulloz

influence of Schiller: 'Subject – historical with a marked preference for Germany in the Middle Ages. Hero – very heroic, and in tragedy, unmistakably guilty. His character is usually free from complications, with no hidden depths. Certain historical combinations occur again and again', is how one critic tartly put it. And the audience was still fragmented. An English visitor to Berlin's theatre commented: 'You see travelling strangers from every country, young people from the middle class when a celebrated actor appears, and on opera nights the upper class, but the real people you never see.'

Of course most of the 'real people' were still in the countryside. In 1850 there were only five towns in German-speaking countries with a population over 100,000. One English gentleman, who was touring through Germany in 1840, described a travelling fair near Frankfurt which was probably typical of the occasional entertainment enjoyed by the 'real people':

'The booths in the fair were devoted to eatables, prints, books and plaster casts, all suited to the lowest class of person. Shooting with an airgun was the favourite amusement – sometimes it was a figure in motion; or else it was a wonderful cottage which opened its doors as soon as it was struck and displayed all of its internal arrangement, from the

cellar to the attic. There was a wonderful troupe of apes from Holland, a circus, a family of acrobats from Hamburg, an Egyptian wizard, a white Negress, a Swiss giantess. In the booth of acrobats I found an elevated stage, a row of musicians in front and several tiers of seats around the circumference. The audience was quiet and observant and much delighted with the jests of Mr. Merryman whose humour was of the very broadest kind.'

The upper class
Since poor communications and lack of mobility curtailed the leisure activities of most people, it is not surprising that the one class that was spectacularly mobile was the aristocracy. Visiting spas in summer and enjoying the hospitality of relatives all over Europe – no matter how remote – were key features of this luxurious way of life.

Because the principalities of Germany had been reduced from more than 300 independent territories in the late 18th century to a mere 39 separate states after the Congress of Vienna in 1815, a class of aristocrats was created who retained their titles but no longer had any territory to rule over. They were known as the 'mediatized princes' and one solution to the difficulty of possessing a noble name but no kingdom, was to travel and stay with one's family –

Well-provisioned picnics – with wine rather than beer – were among the many pursuits enjoyed by Germany's aristocrats who had the time and resources to take their pleasures in the countryside at a gentle pace.

family included not only the most distant cousins, but also their connections via marriage.

So a young, impoverished, mediatized prince could potentially enjoy the hospitality of an extremely extended family. When Prince Chlodwig von Hohenlohe visited Paris he was wined and dined by noble households every night of the week, although he was in no position to reciprocate their hospitality. While in Berlin he dined every week with the King of Prussia himself, whom he regarded as merely his equal in rank. This degree of hospitality could be enjoyed all over Germany, but not in Vienna, where the court remained curiously uninterested in strangers and made little effort. The Prussian military attaché to Vienna, Prince Kraft von Hohenlohe-Ingelfingen, arrived in 1854 and was disappointed to receive almost no invitations in the months that followed. Fortunately, the mobilization of the Austrian army during the Crimean War resulted in a dearth of male dancing partners at balls: 'And so I danced myself rather than introduced myself into the society of Vienna,' he later wrote.

Life in Royal courts
The quality of life in the courts of German-speaking countries varied enormously. Weimar, the capital of Saxe-Meiningen, acquired great cultural prestige because of its association with Goethe, but it remained a town of only 6000 people and many visitors commented on its village-like atmosphere.

At the other end of the scale, Berlin, the capital of Prussia organized its court functions along highly military lines. The guests at a large State function would be divided into categories and entertained according to their rank. For example the women would be grouped as: wives of the nobility; wives of other guests; unmarried girls who had been presented at court; and girls who had not been presented at court. Surprisingly, the formal style of day-to-day life at the Prussian court could also be extremely frugal. Extravagance was only sanctioned on very special occasions, such as a wedding or a Jubilee. At an ordinary dinner, it was quite normal for Kaiser Wilhelm I solemnly to mark with a pen the level of the wine bottle at the end of the meal, before returning it to the cellar in readiness for the next meal.

The impulse towards a cultured life in Germany often came from the middle class, rather than from the court. Schumann discovered this to his cost when he moved from Leipzig, the commercial centre of Saxony, to the relatively dull routine of court life in Dresden, the seat of Saxony's kings. When Mendelssohn arrived in Leipzig in 1835 to take over as musical director of the Gewandhaus, their concerts had already been famous for 50 years, and it was the wealthy textile merchants of Leipzig who subsidized them. In 1843 this commercial patronage also founded a Conservatory, which increased Leipzig's prestige. Goethe and Lessing had been students at the University and Leipzig was also the centre of the growing German publishing industry. All this cultural activity led Goethe to describe the town affectionately as 'der klein Paris' (little Paris).

By contrast, in Dresden many of the most distinguished artists and intellectuals had been drawn from all over Germany to the court of the autocratic King Friedrich Augustus II, where they were smothered by rigid protocol. At first Schumann regarded this dearth of culture as a challenge. 'Here one can get back the old, lost longing for music, there is so little to hear!' he wrote to one friend. But

gradually he was worn down by the spirit of amateurism in the place and after the insurrection in 1849, Schumann left Dresden without regrets.

The hungry years
For many Germans in the early 19th century leisure remained a remote dream. Through railways, industrialization, and Prussia's political ambition, a fragmented and backward territory was slowly turning into the most powerful state in Europe. But the most acute writers of the time all described the process with a premonition that something sinister was happening. Shortly before his death in 1832, Goethe remarked that a war 'like the Thirty Years War' appeared to be imminent.

To some extent commentators were driven by the knowledge that the population was increasing rapidly, without any increase taking place in the supply of food. So pauperism and hunger became more widespread in the 1830s. The following decade was known as 'the hungry forties' because a series of disastrous harvests threatened some areas of the country with famine. One response to this was massive emigration from Germany to the United States. (Perhaps as many as one million Germans emigrated to America between 1820 and 1860.) Another response, in literary terms, was a new type of journalism trying to describe how the poor really lived. Heinrich Bettziech in his description of Berlin wrote in 1846:

'Not a bed nor a table, without firewood, clothes or shoes. No money, no potatoes, no prospects, hope only of the workhouse or a miserable death in the Charité [poor house]. Only rags and straw and dirt and vermin, and hunger howling in their entrails.'

It was a situation that led the poet Heine to sum up German society in the sinister sentences: 'In Germany there are two species of rats: fat rats and hungry rats.' Simple physical survival remained the major preoccupation of most people until well into the 19th century. But then, within a short period from the 1870s to the end of the first decade of the 20th century, the nation was to undergo a remarkable transformation. By 1910, Germany was a wealthy, highly industrialized power.

The artist Georg Kersting has delicately captured the simplicity of life for the middle-class German of this time in his painting The Embroiderer. *The guitar on the sofa hints again at the importance of musical ability as a domestic diversion.*

Contemporary composers

Daniel Auber (1782-1871)

Born in Paris, Auber was sent to England by his father, a courtier of Louis XVI, and returned in 1803 to find his family ruined by the Revolution. After writing some cello concertos, he received instruction from Cherubini, and had his first success with the comic opera *La Bergère Châtelaine* in 1820. There followed a stream of successful operas up to 1869, influenced by Rossini and melodiously simple. One of his few serious operas, *Masaniello,* sparked off the Belgian revolt against the Dutch. He was made director of the Paris Conservatoire in 1842 and *mâitre de chapelle* to Napoleon III in 1852.

Adrien Boieldieu (1775-1834)

Born in Rouen, Boieldieu studied music with the organist of Rouen cathedral and his first opera, *La Fille Coupable,* was produced there in 1793. Moving to Paris, he had a great success with his opera, *La Calife de Bagdad,* in 1800. After an unhappy marriage, he left his post at the Paris Conservatoire to direct the French Opera in St Petersburg until 1811. He returned to have further success, notably with *La Dame Blanche* in 1825, and had a happy second marriage, though troubled in later years by consumptive laryngitis. Although championed by the anti-Rossini faction in French musical circles, Boieldieu was in fact much influenced by Italian music. He was given a state funeral.

Jean-François Le Sueur (1760-1837)

Born near Abbeville in northern France, Le Sueur attended schools there and at Amiens. In 1786 he was appointed choirmaster of Nôtre Dame, Paris, but left after only one year due to disagreements with the clergy. After the Revolution, he became a successful opera composer, rivaling Cherubini. In 1804 Napoleon made him director of the Tuileries chapel; his *Ossian ou Les Bardes* was a major triumph that year. He taught at the newly formed Conservatoire from 1818 and set out his influential ideas on music in *Exposé d'une Musique,* written in retirement.

Giacomo Meyerbeer (1791-1864)

Born Jakob Liebmann Beer in Berlin, the son of a rich banker, Meyerbeer took the name of a relative who had left him a legacy. He studied under Clementi and Vogler before going to Venice, where he was deeply influenced by Rossini. The operas he then wrote were acclaimed in Italy but unsuccessful in Berlin, and in 1826 he moved to Paris, where he met the librettist Scribe. Their collaboration soon produced a run of highly successful operas starting with *Robert le Diable* in 1831. *Les Huguenots* (1836), *Le Prophète* (1849) and *L'Etoile du Nord* (1854), which followed, won great acclaim for their dramatic scenic effects, rather than for their music, but Meyerbeer did not deserve his posthumous neglect.

Jacques Offenbach (1819-80)

Born in Cologne, 'the Mozart of the Champs Elysées' had little success until *Oyayaie* in 1855, the first of many lightweight but entertaining operettas that satirized the follies of the Second Empire. Of these the most famous were *Orphée aux Enfers,* with its notorious cancan (1858), *La Belle Hélène* (1864) and *La Vie Parisienne* (1866). Offenbach's popularity declined after the 1870–71 Franco-Prussian War, and he was forced to tour America in 1876 to restore his finances. His most important work, *The Tales of Hoffman,* was unfinished at his death. In it, he went back to early 19th-century Germany, trying to bridge the gap between serious and light music he had, unwittingly, helped create.

Giovanni Pacini (1796-1867)

Born in Catania, Sicily, the son of an opera singer, Pacini studied at the Bolognese and then the Venetian conservatories before producing his first opera in 1813. A series of successes with Rossini-like operas followed in the decade 1825–35, and he was appointed *Kapellmeister* to the Empress Marie Louise. He retired to Viareggio after a failure in 1835 but re-emerged five years later to enjoy great success with *Saffo* in 1842. Known as the 'master of the cabaleta' he was notoriously attractive to women, even being pursued by a Russian princess.

Bibliography

G. Abraham (ed), *Schumann: A Symposium,* Greenwood, Westport, 1977

J. Barzun, *Berlioz and His Century,* University of Chicago Press, Chicago, 1982

V. Basch, *Schumann,* Ayer & Co., Salem, 1932

R. Carson-Leach, *Berlioz: His Life and Times,* Hippocrene Books, New York, 1984

J. Chissell, *Schumann,* J. M. Dent, London, 1977

J. Chissell, *Schumann Piano Music,* University of Washington Press, Seattle, 1972

A. Desmond, *Schumann Songs,* University of Washington Press, Seattle, 1972

H. Gal, *Schumann Orchestral Music,* University of Washington Press, Seattle, 1980

A. Ganz, *Berlioz in London,* Hyperion, Westport, 1979

F. Hiller, *Mendelssohn: Letters and Recollections,* Vienna House, New York, 1972

J. Horton, *Mendelssohn Chamber Music,* University of Washington Press, Seattle, 1972

D. Jenkins and M. Visocchi, *Mendelssohn in Scotland,* Chappell, London, 1978

S. Kaufman, *Mendelssohn: A Second Elijah,* Greenwood, Westport, 1971

H. Macdonald, *Berlioz,* J. M. Dent, London, 1983

H. Macdonald, *Berlioz Orchestral Music,* University of Washington Press, Seattle, 1969

P. Ostwald, *Schumann: The Inner Voices of a Musical Genius,* Northeastern University Press, Boston, 1985

L. Plantings, *Schumann as Critic,* Da Capo, New York, 1976

B. Primmer, *Berlioz Style,* Da Capo, New York, 1983

P. Radcliffe, *Mendelssohn,* (Master Musician Series), Littlefield, Totowa, 1976

R. Schauffler, *Robert Schumann: The Man and his Music,* Faber and Faber, London, 1976

R. Todd, *Mendelssohn's Early Works for Piano,* Cambridge University Press, Cambridge, 1985

E. Werner, *Mendelssohn: A New Image of the Composer and His Age,* Greenwood, Westport, 1978

Index